Climb th

CW00447649

by John N. Merrill

Maps and photographs by John N. Merrill

1999

Happy Walking International Ltd.

**Happy Walking International Ltd.,
Unit 1, Molyneux Business Park,
Whitworth Road, Darley Dale,
Matlock, Derbyshire, England.
DE4 2HJ**

**Tel/Fax 01629 - 735911
Email - John.Merrill@virgin.net**

Printed, bound, marketed and distributed by Happy Walking International Ltd.

© Text - Walk & Write Ltd. 1999.
© Photographs - Walk & Talk Ltd.1999.
© Maps - Walk & Write Ltd. 1999.

ISBN 1-84173-016-5

British Library Cataloguing-in-Publication Data. A catalogue record of this book is available from the British Library.

Typeset in Comic Sans MS bold, italic, and plain 10pt, 14pt and 18pt,

Please note - The maps in this guide are purely illustrative. You are encouraged to use the appropriate 1:25,000 O.S. map.

Meticulous research has been undertaken to ensure that this publication is highly accurate at the time of going to press. The publishers, however, cannot be held responsible for alterations, errors, omissions, or for changes in details given. They would welcome information to help keep the book up to date.

Cover design and photo -"The summit of Thorpe Cloud" by John N. Merrill - Walk & Talk Ltd © 1999.

ABOUT JOHN N. MERRILL

Few people have walked the earth's crust more than John Merrill with more than 168,000 miles in the last 28 years -the average person walks 75,000 miles in a lifetime. Apart from walking too much causing bones in his feet to snap, like metal fatigue, he has never suffered from any back, hip or knee problems. Like other walkers he has suffered from many blisters, his record is 23 on both feet! He wears out at least three pairs of boots a year and his major walking has cost over £125,000. This includes 87 pairs of boots costing more than £10,200 and over £1,200 on socks - a pair of socks last three weeks and are not washed.

His marathon walks in Britain include - -

Hebridean Journey....... 1,003 miles. Northern Isles Journey......913 miles.
Irish Island Journey ....1,578 miles.   Parkland Journey.......2,043 miles.
Land's End to John o' Groats.....1,608 miles.

and in 1978 he became the first person to walk the entire coastline of Britain - 6,824 miles in ten months.

In Europe he has walked across Austria - 712 miles - hiked the Tour of Mont Blanc, the Normandy coast, the Loire Valley (450 miles), a high level route across the Augverne(230 miles) and the River Seine (200 miles) in France, completed High Level Routes in the Dolomites and Italian Alps, and the GR20 route across Corsica in training! Climbed the Tatra Mountains ,the Transylvanian Alps in Romania, and in Germany walked in the Taunus, Rhine, the Black Forest (Clock Carriers Way) and King Ludwig Way (Bavaria). He has walked across Europe - 2,806 miles in 107 days - crossing seven countries, the Swiss and French Alps and the complete Pyrennean chain - the hardest and longest mountain walk in Europe, with more than 600,000 feet of ascent! In 1998 he walked 1,100 miles along the pilgrimage route from Le Puy (France) to Santiago (Spain) and onto Cape Finisterre.

In America he used The Appalachian Trail - 2,200 miles - as a training walk, before walking from Mexico to Canada via the Pacific Crest Trail in record time - 118 days for 2,700 miles. Recently he walked most of the Continental Divide Trail and much of New Mexico; his second home. In 1999 he walked the Chesopeake & Ohio Canal National Historical Trail. In Canada he has walked the Rideau Trail - Kingston to Ottowa - 220 miles and The Bruce Trail - Tobermory to Niagara Falls - 460 miles.

In 1984 John set off from Virginia Beach on the Atlantic coast, and walked 4,226 miles without a rest day, across the width of America to Santa Cruz and San Francisco on the Pacific coast. His walk is unquestionably his greatest achievement, being, in modern history, the longest, hardest crossing of the U.S.A. in the shortest time - under six months (178 days). The direct distance is 2,800 miles.

Between major walks John is out training in his own area - The Peak District National Park. He has walked all of our National Trails many times - The Cleveland Way thirteen times and The Pennine Way four times in a year! He has been trekking in the Himalayas five times. He created more than thirty-five challenge walks which have been used to raise more than £600,000 for charity. From his own walks he has raised over £100,000. He is author of more than 180 walking guides which he prints and publishes himself, His book sales are in excess of 3 million, He has created many long distance walks including The Limey Way , The Peakland Way, Dark Peak Challenge walk, Rivers' Way, The Belvoir Witches Challenge Walk and the Forest of Bowland Challenge.

3

CONTENTS

INTRODUCTION

Climb the Peaks is a slight misnomer as the Peak District does not, at first sight, have real peaks. The name - The Peak District - originates from the early inhabitants known as Peacs. There are peaks many of which are known as Tors or Pikes. Some have the word Low in them which refer to Saxon times meaning a covering or burial place. But there are some exceptional peaks - notably Shutlingsloe and Chrome Hill.

My aim has been simply to seek out all the "peaks" of the Peak District and ascend each one on a circular walk and traversing the peak. As a result they are all new walks to me. There are several limestone peaks but the majority are gritstone. The views from their summits are exceptional and make the ascent very worth while. The ascents onto Kinder and Bleaklow are more of a moorland climb but their ascents are very mountain like.

I started at Thorpe Cloud the most southern peak, also the smallest, and worked my way northwards. Chrome Hill was a delightful crossing and almost alpine. Bosley Minn as a vantage point over the Cheshire Plain has no equal. Lantern Pike near Hayfield came as a surprise and a lovely little summit. The traverse of Win Hill, Lose Hill and Mam Tor along my "Peakland Ridge" is one of the great walks of the Peak District. The moorland peaks of Kinder and Bleaklow were greatly enjoyed and mostly alone.

I am sad it is all over with for I have enjoyed climbing these peaks and seeing the Peak District from a different perspective. I have climbed them all many times over the years but this book gave me added impetus to go back. Combined from the summits you will see all the Peak District! Despite thousands of miles of walking I never tire of walking the area and still discover paths new to me. Here then are the routes up the main peaks of the Peak District; have a good climb and see you on the summit!

Happy climbing and walking!
John N. Merrill

5

Whilst every care is taken detailing and describing the walk in this book, it should be borne in mind that the countryside changes by the seasons and the work of man. I have described the walk to the best of my ability, detailing what I have found on the walk in the way of stiles and signs. Obviously with the passage of time stiles become broken or replaced by a ladder stile or even a small gate. Signs too have a habit of being broken or pushed over. All the route follow rights of way and only on rare occasions will you have to overcome obstacles in its path, such as a barbed wire fence or electric fence. On rare occasions rights of way are rerouted and these ammendments are included in the next edition.

The seasons bring occasional problems whilst out walking which should also be borne in mind. In the height of summer paths become overgrown and you will have to fight your way through in a few places. In low lying areas the fields are often full of crops, and although the pathline goes straight across it may be more practical to walk round the field edge to get to the next stile or gate. In summer the ground is generally dry but in autumn and winter, especially because of our climate, the surface can be decidedly wet and slippery; sometimes even gluttonous mud!

These comments are part of countryside walking which help to make your walk more interesting or briefly frustrating. Standing in a farmyard up to your ankles in mud might not be funny at the time but upon reflection was one of the highlights of the walk!

The mileage for each section is based on three calculations -

1. pedometer reading.
2. the route map measured on the map.
3. the time I took for the walk.

I believe the figure stated for each section to be very accurate but we all walk differently and not always in a straight line! The time allowed for each section is on the generous side and does not include pub stops etc. The figure is based on the fact that on average a person walks 2 1/2 miles an hours but less in hilly terrain.

High Wheeldon - 422 m.

View from Lantern Pike - 373m - to Kinder Downfall area.

THORPE CLOUD - 287m.

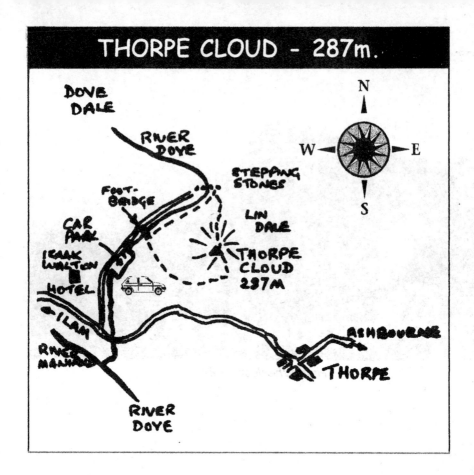

DOVE DALE

RIVER DOVE

STEPPING STONES

FOOT-BRIDGE

LIN DALE

CAR PARK

ISAAK WALTON HOTEL

THORPE CLOUD 287M

ILAM

ASHBOURNE

RIVER MANIFOLD

THORPE

RIVER DOVE

N
W — E
S

Summit of Thorpe Cloud, looking towards Dovedale.

THORPE CLOUD
- 287 metres
- 1 1/2 miles (2.4km)
- 154 metres of ascent.
- allow 1 hour

- 1:25,000 Outdoor Leisure Map No. 24 - The White Peak - East & West sheets.

- Bottom of Dovedale. Grid Ref. SK 148508.

- in the vicinity of Thorpe.

ABOUT THE PEAK - National Trust property, a true peak with steep sides, a magnificent ridge and great views from the summit. Although not quite above 1,000 feet (304.8m) high (mountain height), it is without doubt a rewarding climb at the southern end of the Peak District. In fact gaining the ridge one could almost believe you were on a high summit!

WALKING INSTRUCTIONS - Return to the road from the car park and turn right and walk along it to the stepping stones across the River Dove. Alternatively you can cross a footbridge and walk beside the river on your left to the stepping stones. At the stones turn right - sharp right - and begin ascending the path up the hill. It is rocky in a few places and you soon gain the ridge of the hill and continue ascending to the summit - there is no cairn or triangulation pillar.

For your return you can retrace your steps down or traverse the hill. If traversing continue along the summit area and descend to the right of the ridge to a wall and turn right. Soon picking up a defined path which leads down beneath the flanks of the hill to the footbridge over the River Dove. Cross and turn left back to the car park.

ECTON HILL - 369m.

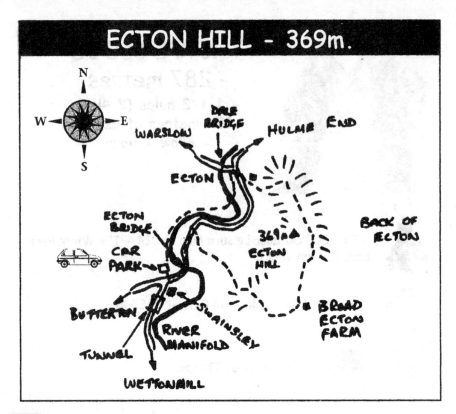

Ecton and the slopes of Ecton Hill - 369m.

ECTON HILL
- 369m
- 180m of ascent
- 3 miles/5 km
- allow more than 1 hour.

Route - Manifold Track - Ecton - Ecton Hill - Broad Ecton Farm - Ecton Bridge - Manifold Track.

- 1:25,000 Outdoor Leisure Map No. 24 - The White Peak - West Sheet.

- Manifold Valley near Ecton Bridge. Grid Ref. SK092578

- None. Nearest at Warslow or Hulme End.

ABOUT THE PEAK - A stunning vantage point, although you don't go all the way to the summit - there is no right of way. The views from the path on the eastern side over the Peak District are extensive. It is a steep ascent and a steeper descent with views of the Manifold Valley. A worthy little hill famed for its copper mines, exploited by the Dukes of Devonshire; the 6th Duke making enough to build The Crescent in Buxton for £120,000!

WALKING INSTRUCTIONS - From the car park beside the Manifold Track/Trail turn right - northwards along it. In less than 1/2 mile after crossing the River Manifold, gain the road to Warslow. Leave the track and turn right to the road junction. Cross to your right to a path sign and track - "Top of Ecton 3/4m". Ascend the track and walk past the house with a copper roof to a stile. Here bear left and ascend steeply up the slopes of Ecton Hill with mine workings to your right. Reach a building at the top and turn right keeping the wall on your left, now ascending more gently to a stile. The path now becomes a magnificent high level traverse with spectacular views left over the Peak District. Reach another wall and bear slightly right away from it to another wall and stile. Through this turn sharp right to a ruined building and a stile. To your right can be seen the triangulation pillar on the summit of Ecton Hill. Through the stile bear slightly left to the next stile and then aim for the lefthand side of the farm buildings - not far left Broad Ecton Farm. Past the farm bear right to a stile and track. Turn right keeping the wall on your right to a path sign. Turn right and cross the field to the far righthand corner. Turn left and keep the wall on your left to a stile. Now you begin the descent, first beside a line of trees on your left. At the end bear right descending by a wall to another. Bearing slightly left continue descending on the path which swings right to a stile and road. Turn left and walk along the road to Ecton Bridge and over it turn right over a stile and follow the path to a footbridge and onto the car park where you began. To your left is Swainsley Hall that you looked down onto as you descended.

The slopes of Ecton Hill - Ecton mine is behind the trees.

Remember and observe the Country Code

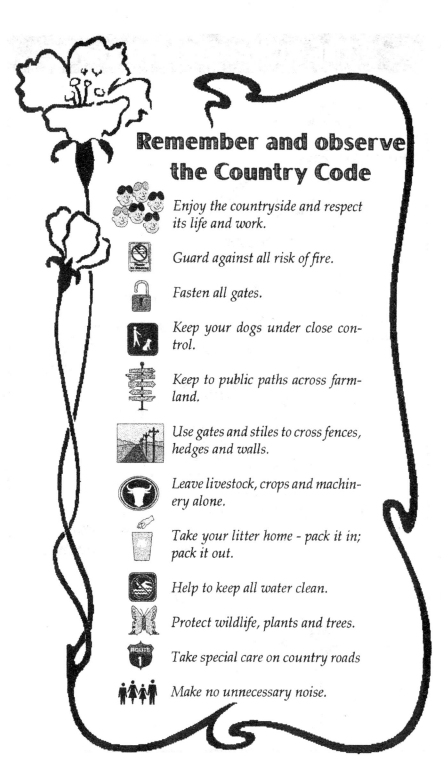

Enjoy the countryside and respect its life and work.

Guard against all risk of fire.

Fasten all gates.

Keep your dogs under close control.

Keep to public paths across farmland.

Use gates and stiles to cross fences, hedges and walls.

Leave livestock, crops and machinery alone.

Take your litter home - pack it in; pack it out.

Help to keep all water clean.

Protect wildlife, plants and trees.

Take special care on country roads

Make no unnecessary noise.

THE ROACHES - 505 m.

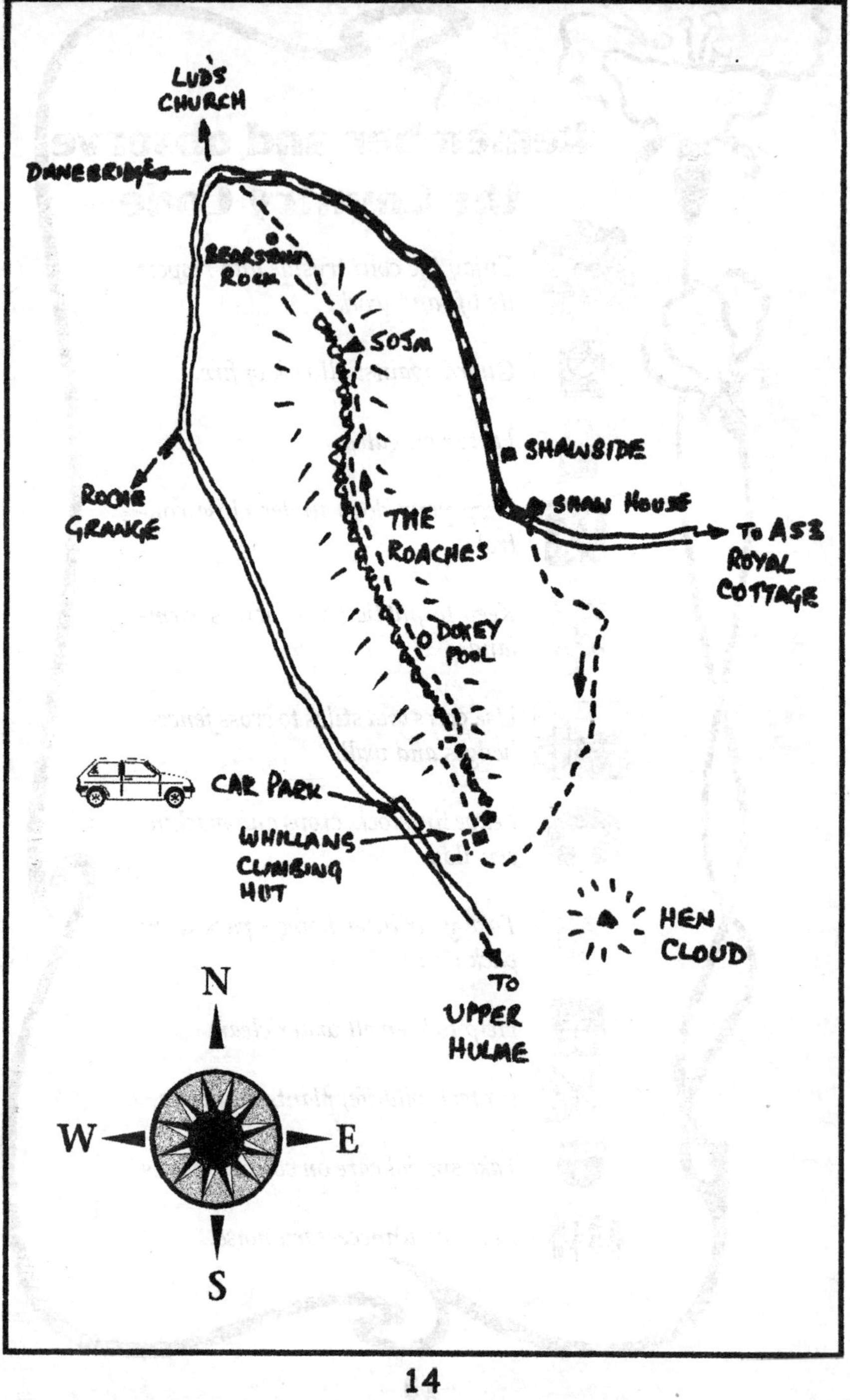

LUD'S CHURCH

DANEBRIDGE

BEARSTONE ROCK

505m

SHAWSIDE

ROCHE GRANGE

SHAW HOUSE

TO A53 ROYAL COTTAGE

THE ROACHES

DOXEY POOL

CAR PARK

WHILLANS CLIMBING HUT

TO UPPER HULME

HEN CLOUD

N
W E
S

THE ROACHES
- 505 m.
- 200 m. of ascent
- 5 MILES
- allow 2 to 3 hours.

Route - The Roaches - Doxey Pool - Trig Point 505m. - Bearstone Rock - Lane - Shaw House - The Roaches.

- 1:25,000 Outdoor Leisure Map - The White Peak - West Sheet.

- Beneath The Roaches. Grid Ref. 004622.

- None. Nearest The Rock, Upper Hulme.

- Roaches Tea Room.

ABOUT THE PEAK- The Roaches has always been a place of fascination and where wallabies are still seen, although their numbers are very depleted. This walk takes along the spine of the rocks and to the highest point as you traverse the peak. A really exceptional vantage point over Staffordshire.

WALKING INSTRUCTIONS - From the car park turn left through the gate and ascend the track towards The Roaches. After a short distance turn left onto a path and soon pass Rockhall - the Don Whillans Memorial Hut - and just past it turn right and ascend to the right of a gritstone buttress and ascend steps to the top. Here turn left and on your left is a stone seat and memorial to the prince and Princess of Teck - August 23rd. 1872. Continue on the path past the highest rock face of the Roaches and approaching a fence turn right and ascend to the top. Here turn left with a wall on your left and walk along the spine of The Roaches. In 1/4 mile pass Doxey Pool on your right. Little over 1/4 mile later pass a concessionary path on your right and less than five minutes later the path bears right to begin the final ascent to the triangulation pillar. Continue onto the trig point and descend the path beyond, on stone slabs and pass Bearstone Rock before gaining the road. The views ahead are worth noting - northwards is moorland above Wildboarclough where a Supermarine Seafire came down. Beyond is the prominent shape of Shutlingsloe where an Airspeed Oxford came down. Both are separate walks for you to do!.

Turn right along the road and ascend at first then descend the road for a mile, passing the other end of the concessionary path and reaching Shaw House on your left turn right, as footpath signed, along a track towards Shawtop. Nearing the house the path has been diverted; turn left and follow the stiles around the lefthand side of the house. Follow the stiled path to a track. Turn right along it and in 200 yards, where it turns left for Summerhill, keep ahead to a gate and follow the path beyond beside the field boundary on your left. This soon brings over the crest with views to Hen Cloud. The path soon becomes a track as you pick up your start out route and regain the road and car park.

The Roaches.

EQUIPMENT NOTES
.... some personal thoughts from John N. Merrill

BOOTS - For summer use and day walking I wear lightweight boots. For high mountains and longer trips I prefer a good quality boot with a full leather upper, of medium weight, with a vibram sole. I always add a foam cushioned insole to help cushion the base of my feet.

SOCKS - I generally wear two thick pairs as this helps minimise blisters. The inner pair are of loop stitch variety and approximately 80% wool. - Thor-lo socks are excellent. The outer are a thick rib pair of approximately 80% wool.

WATERPROOFS - for general walking I wear a T shirt or cotton shirt with a cotton wind jacket on top. You generate heat as you walk and I prefer to layer my clothes to avoid getting too hot. Depending on the season will dictate how many layers you wear. In soft rain I just use my wind jacket for I know it quickly dries out. In heavy or consistant rain I slip on a neoprene lined cagoule, and although hot and clammy it does keep me reasonably dry. Only in extreme conditions will I don overtrousers, much preferring to get wet and feel comfortable. I never wear gaiters!

FOOD - as I walk I carry bars of chocolate, for they provide instant energy and are light to carry. In winter a flask of hot coffee is welcome. I never carry water and find no hardship from not doing so, but this is a personal matter! From experience I find the more I drink the more I want and sweat. You should always carry some extra food such as trail mix & candy bars etc., for emergencies.

RUCKSACKS - for day walking I use a climbing rucksack of about 40 litre capacity and although it leaves excess space it does mean that the sac is well padded, with an internal frame and padded shoulder straps. Inside apart from the basics for one day in winter I carry gloves, balaclava, spare pullover and a pair of socks.

MAP & COMPASS - when I am walking I always have the relevant map - preferably 1:25,000 scale - open in my hand. This enables me to constantly check that I am walking the right way. In case of bad weather I carry a compass, which once mastered gives you complete confidence in thick cloud or mist.

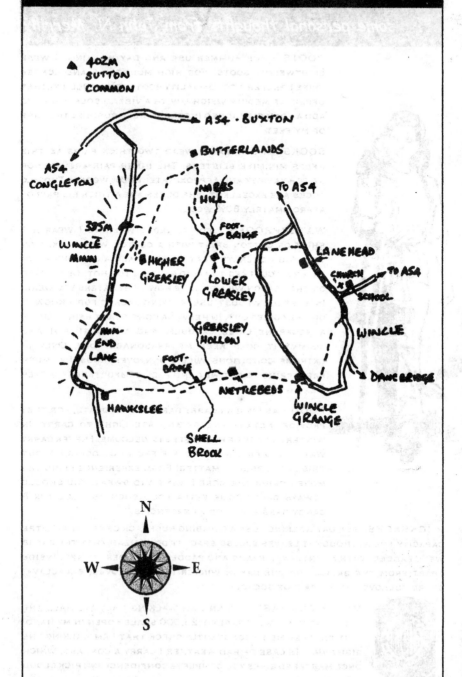

402M
SUTTON
COMMON

A54 · BUXTON

BUTTERLANDS

A54
CONGLETON

NABBS
HILL

TO A54

FOOT-
BRIDGE

LANEHEAD

385M
WINCLE
MINN

HIGHER
GREASLEY

LOWER
GREASLEY

CHURCH

TO A54

SCHOOL

WINCLE

MINN
END
LANE

GREASLEY
HOLLON

FOOT-
BRIDGE

DANE BRIDGE

NETTLEBEDS

HAWKSLEE

WINCLE
GRANGE

SHELL
BROOK

N
W E
S

WINCLE MINN
- 385m
- 150 m of ascent.
- 6 miles 9.6 Km.
- allow 2 to 3 hours.

Route - Wincle - Lanehead Farm - Lower Greasley Farm - Greasley Hollow - Nabbs Hill - Butterlands - Higher Greasley Farm - Wincle Minn - Hawkslee - Nettlebeds - Wincle Grange - Wincle.

- 1:25,000 Outdoor Leisure Map No. 24 - The White Peak - West Sheet.

- None. Limited roadside parking at Wincle, near the church and school.

- None. Nearest 1/2 mile south-east of Wincle at Danebridge.

ABOUT THE PEAK - A real gem; Wincle Minn must be one of the finest ridge walks in England! The views are quite simply stunning. The scenery a delight and you pass the unusually fine Wincle Grange before the hamlet of Wincle. The church, dedicated to St. Michael, is well worth a visit and as you ascend the steps to the door you pass a particularly sad gravestone to the children of the Corbishby family. John died in 1839 aged 18 months; Hannah in 1840 aged 4 years; Joseph in 1840 aged 6 months; and Mary in 1842 aged 1 year. The day I did the walk in March was warm and not a cloud in the sky - summer had come early being in T short and shorts - the skylarks and the curlew sang and the farm drives were adorned with daffodils.

WALKING INSTRUCTIONS - Starting from the church, dedicated to St. Michael, in Wincle, at the road junction, turn right and ascend the lane. In 1/4 mile pass the drive to Lanehead Farm on your left. 100 yards later on your left is a stone stile and trees. Ascend the stile and bear right through the sparse trees and across the field beyond to a stile. Continue ahead to another and onto another by a footpath sign and lane.

The views southwards are to The Roaches. Cross to your right to a cattle grid and descend the track leading down to Greasley Hollow and Lower Greasley Farm. Follow the track round to your right towards the farm but before it turn right over a stile by a path sign. The pathline goes above the farm on your left to a stile on the edge of woodland. Over this descend the path to your right to a footbridge in Greasley Hollow. Ascend the zig-zag path to a stile and then keep to the ridge of Nabbs Hill with beech trees below to your right. Beyond the "summit" of the hill reach a stile. Keep the fence on your left as the path now becomes a track leading to Butterlands.

Before the house turn left on a track - this is a permissive path - and follow the track which soon swings left. Follow it to its end a field later. Here bear slightly right and cross the field to a stile and then onto a gate. Keep the wall on your left as you walk above Higher Greasley Farm. To your right are the final slopes of Wincle Minn. Just past the farm turn right, as footpath signed and follow the grass track which zig-zags up the slope. At the top bear right to the tarmaced surface on the ridge of Wincle Minn. Before turning left - now on the Gritstone Way - turn right to gain the highest point a few yards away. Return and now follow the tarmaced farm road along the ridge with stunning views all around, over Cheshire. Keep on this gated track for more than 1/2 mile following round to your left and descending towards Hawkslee. Where it turn right towards the buildings keep left, as footpath signed, then right to a stile and onto another. Reach another a short distance away on the edge of woodland and a hollow. Continue above this on a grass track to a footpath sign and keep to the lefthand side of the field to a stile and path sign. Continue to another stile and descend more steeply to a stile and woodland. Now descend steeply to a footbridge over Shell Brook. Cross and ascend the field beyond aiming for the righthand side of Nettlebeds.

Gain a track and bear right for a few yards to a stile and path sign on your left. Over this keep the hedge on your left at first before bearing right and ascending towards the righthand side of Wincle Grange. Pass through two stiles and a gate before gaining the lane at the Grange. Turn right and in a few yards left to a gate and footpath sign. Keep the wall on your right to a stile and then cross the next field to the far righthand corner where there is a stile and path sign. Turn right along the lefthand side of the field to a stile and pathsign before the Danebridge lane. Turn left and descend to Wincle church where you began.

WINCLE GRANGE - Originally belonged to Combermere Abbey in Cheshire and has ecclesiastical style windows.

View to Wincle Minn.

Wincle Grange.

HIGH WHEELDON - 422m.

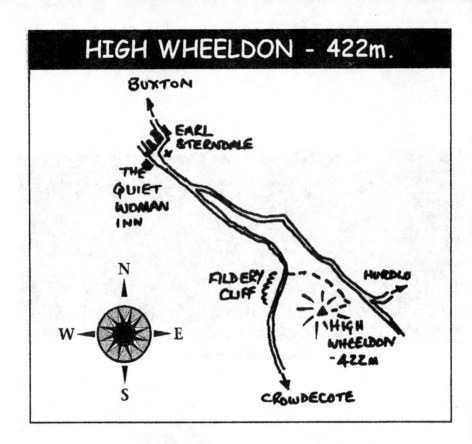

View from High Wheeldon to Chrome Hill.

HIGH WHEELDON
- 422m
- 152m of ascent.
- 1 1/2 miles - 2.4 km.
- allow 1 hour.

 - 1:25,000 Outdoor Leisure Map No. 24 - The White Peak - West Sheet.

 - None. Roadside parking beside Aldery Cliff.

 - The Quiet Woman, Earl Sterndale - 3/4 mile from route.

ABOUT THE PEAK - A delightful hill above the upper reaches of the River Dove. The hill was given to the National Trust in 1946 and a plaque on the triangulation pillar commemorates the people killed during the second World War. Aldery Cliff is a good limestone climbing cliff, managed by the B.M.C. (British Mountaineering Council).

WALKING INSTRUCTIONS - From Aldery Cliff ascend eastwards over the stile close to the National Trust sign and ascend the path around the northern side of the hill. After little more than 1/4 mile you come to a stile on your left and a path sign. Turn right and ascend steeply up a path aiming for the summit and triangulation pillar. The views are extensive especially to Parkhouse Hill and Chrome Hill. Retrace your steps back to Aldery Cliff.

Trig point in the summit of High Wheeldon.

CHROME HILL - 440 m.

CHROME HILL
- 440 metres
- 300 m. of ascent.
- 5 miles - 8 km.
- allow 2 hours.

Basic Route - Hollinsclough - Stannery - Chrome Hill - Stoop Farm - Booth Farm - Fough - Hollinsclough.

- 1:25,000 Outdoor Leisure Map - The White Peak - West Sheet.

- None. Roadside parking in Hollinsclough.

- None nearest at Longnor 2 miles SE. Tearoom at Dowall Hall; little over 1/4 mile from the start of Chrome Hill - great views of the hill and of Parkhouse Hill obtained from here!

ABOUT THE WALK - Chrome Hill is one of the finest "peaks" of the Peak District and until recently you were not allowed to ascend, as there was no right of way. Now there is a Concessionary path along its spine making it one of the finest traverses in the Peak. You traverse the limestone mountain and return through gritstone country back to Hollinsclough. Both Chrome Hill and Parkhouse Hill are very interesting geologically being limestone reef knolls.

WALKING INSTRUCTIONS - From the cross roads in Hollinsclough, with a Methodist Chapel to your left dated 1801, walk eastwards down the lane past the village school with bell tower dated 1840. (The road on your left at the start is your return route.) In less than 1/4 mile the lane turns right and here on your left is a path sign, track, cattle grid and barn. Follow the track to another path sign in 200 yards and turn right following the track and descending to a ford crossed by a footbridge on its right. Continue ahead on the track and soon pass Stannery Farm to your right and gain the lane from Glutton Bridge with Parkhouse Hill in front of you. Turn left along the lane and in a few yards you can see a tablet on the side of Parkhouse Hill - "In loving memory of Frank Holland of Glutton Grange - 1921 - 1994." Continue along the lane, which goes through Dowel Dale, to a cattle grid and turn left, as footpath signed - Chrome Hill. Dowall Hall Tearoom is straight ahead along the lane.

The path, which is defined, immediately starts ascending the slopes of Chrome Hill; continue ascending to its limestone summit ridge. The views are superb all over as you ascend. Gaining the ridge the path weaves its way between the limestone buttresses as you gradually descend along its spine. At the end turn left to a stile and turn right along the lefthand side of the field. To your left can be seen the limestone Swallow Tor above Swallow Brook. At the next stile and nearing Tor Rock bear right and ascend to a wall and turn left walking beside it with the Tor to your left. Keep beside the wall to the farm track to Stoop Farm. Cross over and as footpath signed follow the path "To Booth Farm." To your left is Stoop Farm. The path goes diagonally half left across the fields and after the first one keep the wall on your left and in 200 yards gain a stile and track. Bear right along it as it curves left to Booth Farm. At the entrance to the farm keep straight ahead on the track signed for Fough. You are now in gritstone country. The track descends to Fough and you keep to the lefthand side of it and continue descending the track. Little over 1/4 mile from Fough the track curves left and as footpath signed you leave it and descend to your right to a footbridge over a stream. Ascend to your left close to the lefthand side of the field to a walled path and gate before the road to Hollinsclough. Turn left and descend into the village.

Chrome Hill - southern end.

Chrome Hill - western side.

Parkhouse Hill from the slopes of Chrome Hill.

27

SHUTLINGSLOE - 506 m.

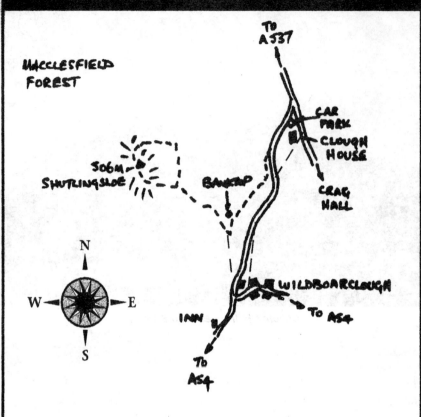

MACCLESFIELD
FOREST

TO
A537

CAR
PARK

CLOUGH
HOUSE

506M
SHUTLINGSLOE

BANKTOP

CRAG
HALL

N
W E
S

WILDBOARCLOUGH

TO A54

INN

TO
A54

Group of fellow walkers on the summit of Shutlingsloe.

SHUTLINGSLOE
- 506 m
- 200 m. of ascent
- 4 MILES/7 km
- allow 2 hours

Route - *Clough House Car Park - Banktop - Shutlingsloe - Banktop - Wildboarclough - Clough House - Car Park.*

- 1:25,000 Outdoor Leisure Map No. 24 - The White Peak - West Sheet.

- Clough House Car Park. Grid Ref. 988698.

- Just off the route in Wildboarclough - Crag Inn.

ABOUT THE PEAK - An outstanding little walk to the summit of one of true peaks of the Peak District. The walk loops around the summit before descending to Wildboarclough. The hamlet is most attractive where the impressive mill was once the Post Office. The valley was severally flooded on May 24th 1989 and you will see a plaque to this and see several bridges being that date, having been rebuilt. The village also won the 1995 "Best Village" award.

WALKING INSTRUCTIONS - From the car park return to the main road and turn left along it. In less than 1/4 mile, just after passing a pathsign and footbridge on your left to Clough House - your return route - turn right at the pathsign - Langley and Shutlingsloe. The path gently ascends to your left above the road to Banktop House. Pass it on its left side and gain the track. Follow it to a junction and path sign for Shutlingsloe, near a cattle grid. Turn right and ascend the track and where it turns right for Shutlingsloe Farm, bear left as signed with a wall on your right. Ascend to a stile as the ascent becomes more pronounced. The path ahead to the summit is your descent path! Turn right on a mostly level path with a wall to your right. In 1/4 mile reach a ladder stile. Over this the path bears left as you walk through a shallow clough. At the top continue ahead to a wall and the path junction with the summit path to your left and right over the moor to Macclesfield Forest. Turn left and ascend to the summit of

Shutlingsloe. On the summit is a plaque to Arthur Smith a footpath fighter. The views from here are extensive.

From the summit descend steeply down the path you looked up as you ascended the hill. Soon regain your earlier path and retrace it to the track junction. Here turn right along the track and descend to the main road. To your right is the Crag Inn. Turn left then right passing the flood disaster plaque. Ascend past the old mill and before St. Saviour church, turn left, as footpath signed along a track. This leads past the church to a row of cottages. Walk past them - above to your right is mill pond. Descend to the minor road and turn right. Follow the road for more 1/4 mile seeing the bridges and embankments following the 1989 flood. Pass your path to Shutlingsloe and turn right over the footbridge, by the path sign. Follow the path to the righthand side of Clough House. Reaching the farm road turn left back into the car park.

Former Post Office in Wildboarclough.

View from summit down to Wildboarclough.

View to Shutlingsloe from near Birchenclough Hill.

TEGG'S NOSE - 350 m.

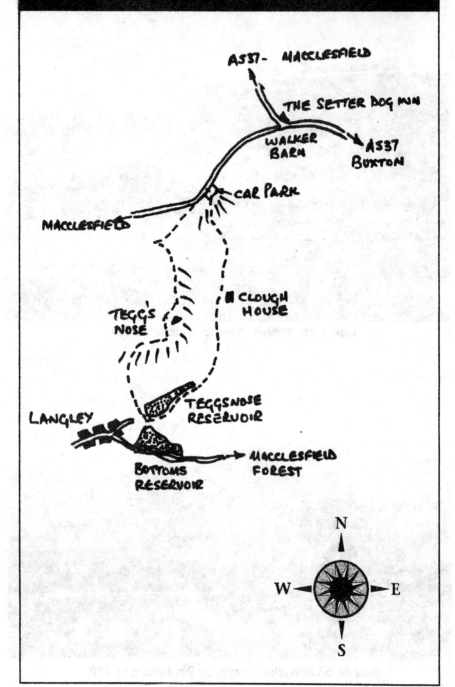

A537- MACCLESFIELD

THE SETTER DOG INN

WALKER BARN

A537 BUXTON

CAR PARK

MACCLESFIELD

CLOUGH HOUSE

TEGG'S NOSE

TEGGSNOSE RESERVOIR

LANGLEY

BOTTOMS RESERVOIR

MACCLESFIELD FOREST

N
W E
S

TEGG'S NOSE
- 350 m.
- 145 metres of ascent
- 3 miles / 4.8 km.
- allow one hour or more.

 - 125,000 Outdoor Leisure Map No. 24 - The White Peak - West Sheet.

 - Tegg's Nose Country Park - Windy Way - 1/2 mile from Walkers Barn (The Setter Dog Inn) on the A537. Grid Ref. SK948733.

 - Nearest on A537, The Setter Dog.

 Refreshments, Toilets and Information at car park.

ABOUT THE PEAK - Stunning views over Cheshire and Langley from its summit area - there is a viewing plaque on the southern edge - over Langley. The hill is a former gritstone quarry with various items of machinery with information plaques still in place. The Gritstone Trail passes through and is followed for the ascent. Unlike the other "Peaks" in this book you start at the top! First descending to Teggnose Reservoir before ascending to its summit - the views make it worthwhile with the impressive true peak of Shutlingsloe lying more than three miles south east of here. Much of the route follows the signed Tegg's Nose Trail.

WALKING INSTRUCTIONS - From the car park walk to the edge and view and descend the Saddlers Way, a cobbled track along the line of an old packhorse route. At the bottom bear right along a tarmaced road towards Clough House. Just before it turn right and follow the track to a stile and continue ahead to stepping stones before walking around the southern side of Teggsnose Reservoir. From here you have impressive views of the "hill". At the end of the reservoir turn right along its wall to a small parking area. Go through the kissing gate on the left - now on the Gritstone Trail - and begin ascending the steps up Ward's Knob. Where the slope eases the path bears right and continues ascending to the track around the summit area. Go over the stile and turn right and almost immediately left and follow a small path keeping to the highest ground. The path encircles above the quarry face and provides a good vantage point over Cheshire. Follow the path round and down to a kissing gate and turn right along the track/path back to the road and entrance to the car park.

Teggsnose Reservoir and Tegg's Nose.

OBSERVE THE MOUNTAIN CODE

1. Plan, with maps.

2. Don't try too much too soon. Move gradually to bigger things.

3. Go with others and keep together always. Until experienced don't take charge of others: then take only ten or less.

4. Equip against the worst. Be well shod: have warm clothing and a waterproof cover, spare clothes and food for all, map, whistle, torch and compass.

5. Give yourself ample time, and more as a reserve. Move steadily. Don't hurry and don't waste time.

6. Don't throw down or dislodge rocks or stones. Know and observe the Country Code.

7. Eye the weather it can change completely in a few hours. Don't go on recklessly if it turns bad. Don't be afraid to come down.

8. Don't go rock, snow or ice climbing without an experienced leader.

9. If lost don't panic or rush down. Keep together and deliberately work out your position and your best way down.

10. Leave word behind you of your route and when you expect to be back. If you arrive where friends don't expect you, 'phone them or tell the police (to save needless searches).

SHINING TOR - 559 m.

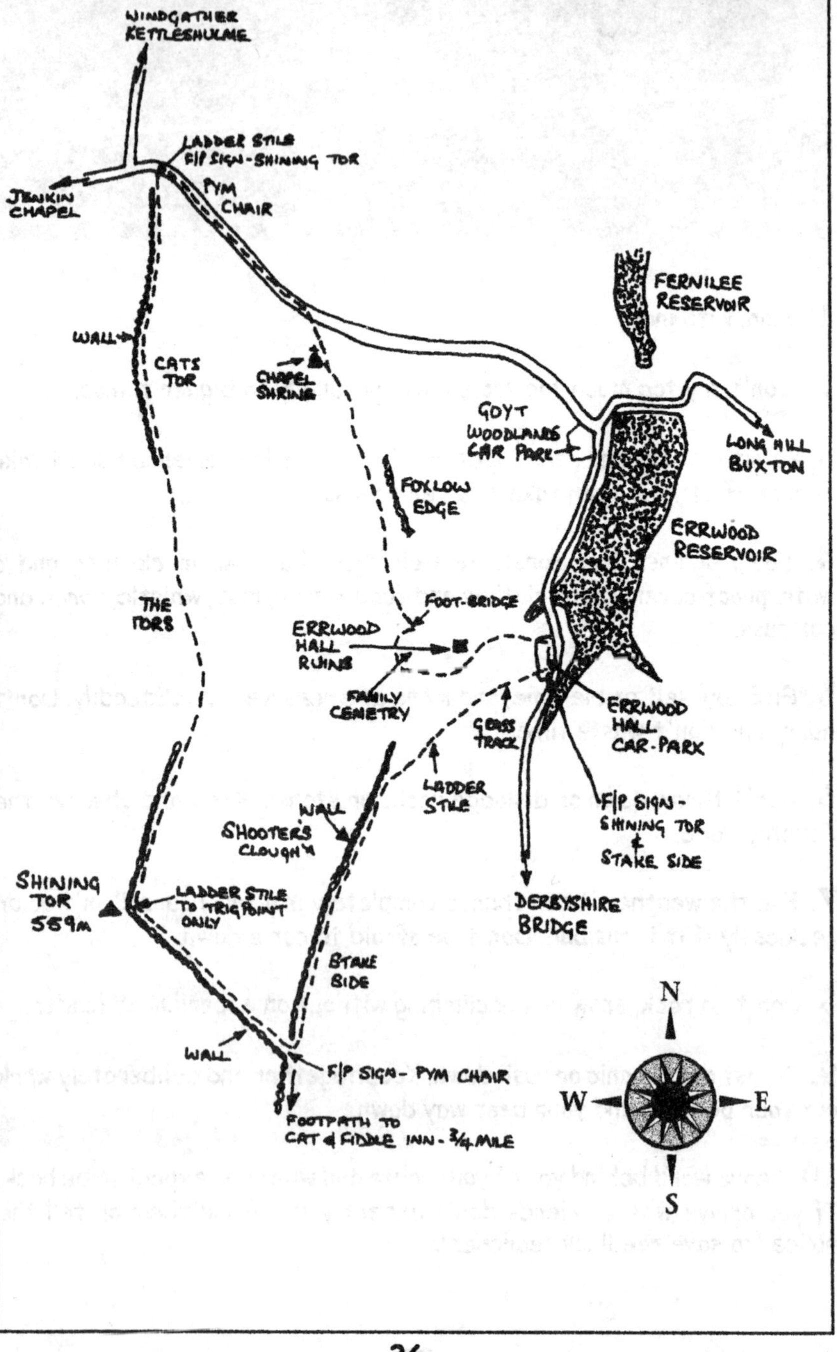

WINDGATHER
KETTLESHULME

LADDER STILE
F/P SIGN - SHINING TOR

JENKIN
CHAPEL

PYM
CHAIR

FERNILEE
RESERVOIR

WALL

CATS
TOR

CHAPEL
SHRINE

GOYT
WOODLANDS
CAR PARK

LONG HILL
BUXTON

FOXLOW
EDGE

ERRWOOD
RESERVOIR

THE
TORS

FOOT-BRIDGE

ERRWOOD
HALL
RUINS

FAMILY
CEMETERY

GRASS
TRACK

ERRWOOD
HALL
CAR-PARK

LADDER
STILE

F/P SIGN -
SHINING TOR
&
STAKE SIDE

WALL

SHOOTERS
CLOUGH

SHINING
TOR
559m

LADDER STILE
TO TRIG POINT
ONLY

STAKE
SIDE

DERBYSHIRE
BRIDGE

WALL

F/P SIGN - PYM CHAIR

FOOTPATH TO
CAT & FIDDLE INN - 3/4 MILE

N
W   E
S

SHINING TOR
- 559 m
- 300 m of ascent
- 6 miles / 7 km.
- allow 2 1/2 hours.

Route - Errwood Hall car park - Stake Side - Shining Tor - The Tors - Cats Tor - Pym Chair - Errwood Shrine - Errwood Hall (ruins) - car park.

 - O.S. 1:25,000 Outdoor Leisure Map No. 24 - The White Peak - west sheet.

 - Errwood Hall.

 - None. Nearest - Cat & Fiddle Inn - 3/4 mile south of the route, before Shining Tor.

ABOUT THE PEAK & WALK - a high moorland walk which is best appreciated in good weather to visibly see the route and enjoy the extensive views.   The walk can be extended from the path junction near Shining Tor to visit the Cat and Fiddle Inn - one of the highest in the country - 3/4 mile away. The walk from Shining Tor is down a broad ridge with impressive views and is basically downhill all the way back to Errwood Hall car park. The hardest part is the initial ascent to Shining Tor.

WALKING INSTRUCTIONS - From the lefthand (southern end) of the car park pick up the signed path - Shining Tor and Stake Side. The path is well defined and soon becomes a grass track as you ascend gradually, with woodland on your left. After almost 1/2 mile ascend a ladder stile and soon gain a wall on your right. Keep close to this as you bear left continuing your ascent up the shoulder of Stake Side. Over the wall and below is Shooter's Clough. After nearly a mile beside the wall reach a footpath junction. The path ahead is to the Cat and Fiddle Inn and the path on your right, as signed - Pym Chair - leads you towards the summit of Shining Tor. Keep the wall on your left to the summit. Access to the triangulation pillar is via the stile. The nearby southern slopes are a popular hand gliding area.

Continue along the path with the wall on your left as you now gently descend along the ridge over The Tors and Cats Tor to the road at Pym Chair, 1 1/2 miles away. Turn right along the road for 1/2 mile before turning onto the path and continue descending beneath Foxlow Edge, passing the small circular shrine on your right. The path is well defined for the next 3/4 mile with the stream on your right. After 3/4 mile turn right over the footbridge and ascend the path, which soon joins a track where you turn left down it. Just off to your left is the Grimshawe cemetery. After 200 yards the track divides; to your left round the corner are the ruins of Errwood Hall. The one ahead continues through the rhododendrons, which are particularly attractive in June when in full bloom. After a few yards bear right at the next junction and you soon emerge into the field above the car park. Descend back to your starting point.

ERRWOOD HALL - built by Samuel Grimshaw in 1830, whose estate covered 496 acres. The Grimshaw's planted over 40,000 azaleas and rhododendrons in the area and accounts for the extensive foliage today. The building was Italian style with a large central tower. In 1930 the building was purchased by Stockport Corporation and for a short while served as a Youth Hostel before being pulled down in 1934 with the building of Fernilee Reservoir.

CIRCULAR SHRINE - Built by the Grimshaw family in 1889 in memory of their Spanish governess. The shine is dedicated to St. Joseph.

ERRWOOD RESERVOIR - Completed in 1967 for the Stockport and District Water Board, and has a holding capacity of 927 million gallons. The neighbouring Fernilee Reservoir was completed in 1938 and has a capacity of 1,087 million gallons.

View across Shooter's Clough to Shining Tor.

Cat & Fiddle Inn sign.

KERRIDGE HILL - 313 m.

GRITSTONE TRAIL

WHITE NANCY

GOOSE FARM

N
W — E
S

SUGAR LANE

B5470 KETTLESHULME

KERRIDGE HILL

RAINOW

SCHOOL

HOLY TRINITY

313m

TOWER HILL FOLLY

B5470 MACCLESFIELD

Monument on White Nancy.

From opposite page -
ridge of Saddle of Kerridge to a stile
on your left. Then keep the wall on your
right as you walk along the spine to more
stiles and onto the triangulation pillar -
313m - and views of the Cheshire Plain.
Continue ahead soon descending to a
stile and on down a wide path to a track
junction. Here turn left and walk beside a wall on your right and in less than
1/4 mile bear right to a stile and walled
path. Descend this and bear right to
pass the ruins of a mill on your left and
ascend the path to the B5470 at Tower
Hill, gained via a stile by a footpath
signed. Turn left and soon pass Tower
Hill folly on your left and walk up the
road back to Holy Trinity church.

KERRIDGE HILL
- 313 m.
- 115 metres of ascent.
- 4 miles / 6.4 km.
- allow 1 1/2 hours.

 - 1:25,000 Outdoor Leisure Map No. 24 - The White Peak - West Sheet.

 - No official one. Roadside parking in Rainow.

 - Off the route in Rainow - The Robin Hood Inn.

ABOUT THE PEAK - Rainow in Cheshire near Bollington borders the Peak National Park. The Saddle of Kerridge, part of the Gritstone Trail, has long been a favourite of mine and lies just outside the Peak National Park boundary. Although the western side is quarried the ridge itself is stunning and is the last high ground before the Cheshire Plain. The views are superb. Before the final ascent to White Nancy and the hill I passed a farm selling goose eggs. There was an honesty box on the goose enclosure. For 20p each (1999 price) I bought two eggs and carried them over the hill and had them for breakfast the next day! You walk along the ridge to the triangulation point before descending back to Rainow, in doing so traversing the complete hill.

WALKING INSTRUCTIONS - Starting from Rainow Church dedicated to Holy Trinity descend the road on your left - Round Meadow - passing the school as the road bears right. Soon afterwards turn left along Sugar Lane and follow the lane for 1/4 mile to a small reservoir on your left. Pass a waterfall on your left and a house on your right. Just after turn right to a gate and stile. Ascend the path to your right to join another and turn right along the level contouring path to a gap in the field edge. Keep ahead on the path to a stile and onto the "goose" farm. Just beyond gain a track and turn left - now on the Gritstone Trail. Above to your left is the white monument on White Nancy - your first goal. Continue ascending the lane to near its summit and turn left, as Gritstone Trail footpath signed, and ascend the steps and path to the white monument. Here the views unfold with Manchester Airport to the north. Keep along the

41

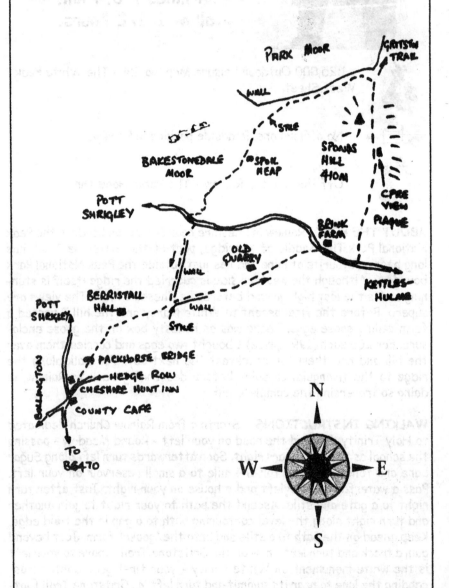

SPONDS HILL
- 410 m
- 215 m of ascent.
- 6 miles / 9.6 km.
- allow 2 1/2 hours.

- 1:25,000 Outdoor Leisure Map No. 24 - The White Peak - West sheet
- No 1 - The Dark Peak - West sheet.

- No official one. Roadside parking on the lane to Pott Shrigley between the Cheshire Hunt Inn and County Cafe.

- Cheshire Hunt Inn, at start/end of the walk.

- County Cafe at start/end of the walk.

ABOUT THE PEAK - You follow a section of the Gritstone trail to the summit area before returning over the moors back to the Pott Shrigley lane. Unlike the other walks/climbs in this guide you do not actually gain the summit as it lies just off the route. The CPRE in 1975 have put a viewing plaque at the highest point of the path which gives an incredible 360° degree view. The hill is the last vantage point before the Dark Peak massif.

WALKING INSTRUCTIONS - Starting from the Pott Shrigley road close to Cheshire Hunt Inn, turn right up Hedge Row and pass the inn on your left. Just after turn left over a stile - you are following the Gritstone Trail - and cross the field guided by posts before descending to a miniature packhorse bridge over Harrop Brook. Cross this to a stile and then ascend to the end of a wall where there is a gap. Continue ahead for a few yards before bearing right over a natural bridge and ascend the field to the right of Berristall Hall. Aim for the top lefthand corner of a wall - it is Gristone Trail signed - and walk along the edge of the beech trees beside a wall on your right. This soon becomes a walled track to a stile. Here continue ahead with the wall on your right - to your left is your return path. Impressive views to your left now unfold. Reach a cattle grid and track cross and leave it on your left to a stile. Keep ahead soon with a wall on your right. Soon with an old quarry on your left bear right and diagonally cross the field to a stile and keep straight ahead with the path soon becoming a track as you approach the minor road before Brink Farm.

At the road turn right passing the farm on your left and in less than 1/4 mile turn left over the stile by a path sign - you are still on the Gritstone Trail. Continue ascending and in more than 1/4 mile reach the CPRE viewing plaque on your right. Continue on the track and to your left is the triangulation pillar on the top of Sponds Hill. 1/4 mile from the viewing plaque leave the Gritstone Trail and turn left along a path which soon keeps close to the wall on your right. The views to your right are over Lyme Park. In 1/4 mile the track leaves the wallside and your follow it to your left to a stile. Continue ahead to an overgrown spoil heap - this was a coal mining area and you will see the capped shafts to your right, soon. At the heap bear left and continue on a grass track descending to a ladder stile. Over this follow the track down over Bakestonedale Moor to the minor road to Pott Shrigley. Turn left over the bridge over the brook and in a few yards right to a stile and path sign. Ascend with the wall on your right and then across level ground with the wall on your right to the stile you used earlier. Turn right and descend through the beech trees - now back on the Gritstone Trail - and pass Berristall Hall to your right and retrace your steps back to packhorse bridge and on to the Cheshire Hunt Inn and County Cafe.

Sponds Hill (left skyline) and panorama plaque (right).

The Sett Valley Trail.

View to Lantern Pike (centre).

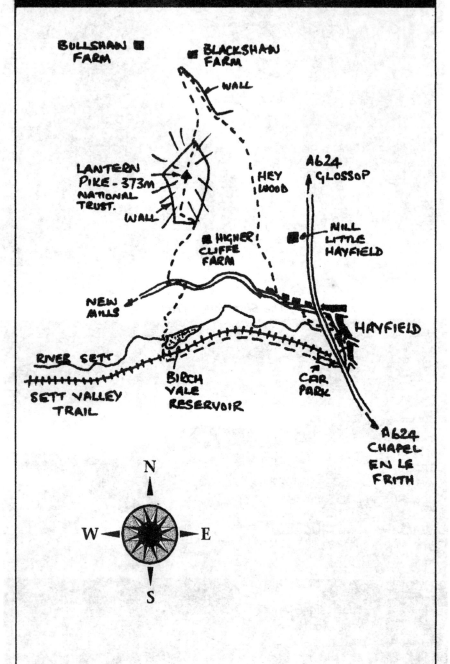

BULLSHAW FARM

BLACKSHAW FARM

WALL

LANTERN PIKE - 373m NATIONAL TRUST.

WALL

HEY WOOD

A624 GLOSSOP

MILL LITTLE HAYFIELD

HIGHER CLIFFE FARM

NEW MILLS

HAYFIELD

RIVER SETT

BIRCH VALE RESERVOIR

CAR PARK

A624 CHAPEL EN LE FRITH

SETT VALLEY TRAIL

N
W   E
S

LANTERN PIKE
- 373m
- 193 m of ascent.
- 5 miles/8 Km.
- allow 2 hours.

Route - Hayfield - Sett Valley Trail - Lantern Pike, 373m - Blackshaw Farm - Little Hayfield - Hayfield.

- 1:25,000 Outdoor Leisure Map No. 1 - The Dark Peak - West sheet.

- Hayfield - Sett Valley Trail.

- Packhorse Inn, Royal Hotel, George Hotel, Bull's Head, Kinder Lodge Inn, Hayfield.

- Twenty Trees Cafe, Hayfield.

ABOUT THE PEAK - Exceptional peak with 360° views from the rocky summit; especially to Kinder Scout and the Downfall area. The summit has a Hill Indicator to the outlying hills and is in Memory of Edwin Royce - 1880 - 1946. The hill is National Trust property. From below and until the final stages of the ascent, Lantern Pike does not appear a high summit but dwarfed by the hill to its west; but it is when you get there! In about 40 minutes from the car park you should be on the summit!

WALKING INSTRUCTIONS - From the car park at Hayfield at the start of the 2 1/2 mile Sett Valley Trail, follow the trail for nearly 3/4 mile. After a third of a mile cross Slacks Crossing and in another third to your right is Birch Vale Reservoir with Lantern Pike beyond. Continue on the trail to the end of the reservoir to a factory on your right, and turn right, as footpath signed and descend to the western end of the reservoir. Cross it via a footbridge and over the River Sett to a stile. Continue to another with signs - "Dogs not on a lead will be shot". Continue ascending to another stile, path sign and track. Turn left along it and in a 100 yards turn right and continue ascending the track to the minor road to

Thornsett. Turn right then left beside No. 5 Windy Knowle, and ascend the bridlepath signed tarmaced lane. Pass the turning to your right to Higher Cliffe Farm and pass a house on your left. Just after the tarmaced surface becomes a track and continue ascending to a gate and enter Lantern Pike, National Trust property.

Turn left by the wall on your left and ascend to the right of the pike. Turn right and ascend to the summit and Hill Indicator. After admiring the view over Kinder and down to Hayfield and beyond, continue your traverse of the pike and descend to a walled track. Continue to a gate and cross the field on a track with Highland cattle grazing. Gaining the far righthand corner of the field with Blackshaw Farm beyond, turn right almost back on yourself, and keep the wall on your left, as footpath signed. In 1/4 mile reach a stile with woodland - Hay Wood (beech and pine) - on your left and begin descending to another stile and pass footpath sign No. 89 - Hayfield. Just after pass Firbob Cottage on your right and keep ahead on the track with Little Hayfield Mill below to your left. Continue to a gate and onto another. Here the path forks and keep to the lefthand one to descend to a mill and gain Bank Vale Road. Continue along the road to the Thornsett/Hayfield lane beside Oaklands on your right. Turn left along the lane and in 50 yards turn right and follow the path by the River Sett and pass under the A624 Glossop Road to emerge into central Hayfield opposite the Packhorse Inn. Turn right along Market Street and just after the church turn right, as footpath signed - Sett Valley - and soon turn left to walk through the underpass to emerge back at Sett Valley Car Park.

SETT VALLEY TRAIL - Built for the Midland and Great Central Joint Railway Company in 1868. The railway closed in 1970 and three years later work began to convert it to a pedestrian way.

Lantern Pike cairn and view to Kinder Scout.

48

View to Crow Chin and High Neb.

Millstones beneath High Neb.

HIGH NEB - 458 m.

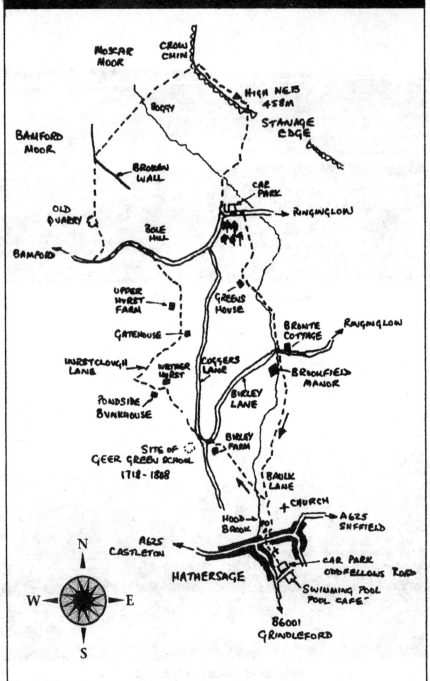

HIGH NEB
- 458m
- 330m of ascent
- 8 miles/13 Km
- allow 3 hours

Route - Hathersage - Cliff Wood - Birley Farm - Nether Hurst - Hurstclough Lane - Gatehouse - Bolehill - Old Quarry - Bamford Moor - Moscar Moor - Crow Chin - High Neb 458m - Stanage Edge - Dennis Knoll - Green's House - Bronte Cottage - Baulk Lane - Hathersage.

- 1:25,000 Outdoor Leisure Map No. 1 - The Dark Peak - East Sheet.

- Off Oddfellows Road; opposite Hathersage Swimming Pool, gained from the B6001 road. Grid Ref. SK233815.

- Several in Hathersage including Hathersage Inn and Little John Inn.

- Pool Cafe and others in Hathersage.

ABOUT THE PEAK AND WALK - First you gently meander and ascend to Bamford Moor. From here, whilst you can see your objective a compass bearing is useful. The summit of High Neb is a magnificent viewpoint with 360° views. The descent is more direct back to Hathersage. The walk has literary associations for you pass the site of Geer Green School, the first in the area, between 1718 - 1808 and was in Jane Eyre's village of Morton. As you descend you pass the aptly named Bronte Cottage. In Hathersage you pass a former Button factory. On Stanage Edge you will see many abandoned millstones and see water channels cut into rock and numbered. You will also see some climbers!

WALKING INSTRUCTIONS - From the car park exit its bottom righthand corner where there is a kissing gate and walk past Hathersage Methodist church to the A625 road in Hathersage. Cross to your right and pass the Post Office and walk up Besom Lane with three storied building - a former button factory - to Baulk Lane. Turn left and soon pass the cricket field (teas served on Saturdays) and the house - Riverside. Just after turn left and descend the field to the right to a footbridge - you return via Baulk Lane. Cross the bridge and cross the drive of Brookfield Manor, and ascend the path to the right through the trees of Cliff Wood to a stile. Continue ascending towards Birley Farm walking around the righthand side of it, guided by stiles, to Birley Lane. Turn left to the lane junction with Coggers Lane and turn right; just opposite is a plaque on the gatepost recording the site of Geer Green School. Ascend Coggers Lane for a short distance to a gate and footpath sign on your left. Keep to the righthand side of the field by the row of trees and descend to a gate and footbridge. After this ascend towards Nether Hurst and a stile. Here gain a track and turn left and walk past Poolside Bunkhouse on your left and gain a walled path. Follow this to a junction less than 1/4 mile away. Turn right, now on Hurstclough Lane - a walled track - and follow this for more than 1/4 mile towards the Gatehouse. Where the track turns right to the house on your left is a stile. Go through and ascend straight ahead guided by stiles passing Upper Hurst Farm to your left to a stile and woodland. Turn right then left following a contouring path to the lane beneath Bole Hill. For much of the ascent you have had magnificent views westwards over the Hope Valley.

At the lane turn left and walk along it down to a hollow and ascend to the brow of the rise - 1/4 mile of road walking altogether. Here on the otherside is a ladder stile on your right. Ascend and follow the defined path round to an old quarry. Keep to the righthand side of it before heading due north for 1/4 mile to the corner of a partially ruined wall. From here north - north - easterly is Crow Chin and High Neb. The path line is faint over Bamford Moor to Crow Chin so unless in fog when a compass bearing is useful (50°) aim for Crow Chin. You will need to bear left after a 1/3 mile to avoid the drainage area of Hood Brook. Ascend to the path/track beneath Crow Chin. Bear right then left and ascend the path to the top of the gritstone outcrop and turn right to the triangulation pillar on High Neb. Here are the views and great sweep of Stanage Edge. Walk along the top for a short distance to the end of main rock faces and descend the path down past numerous millstones. Cross the path/track beneath the edge and continue on the defined path leading down to a ladder stile and the track - Long Causeway. Continue down the track to road beside a car parking area.

Turn left along the road to a cattle grid and turn right and follow the path beside a wall on your right. Follow the path which lower down turns right to a stile and then left to Green's House. Turn left then right through a stile and continue descending guided by stiles to woodland and a foot bridge. Cross and walk down the lefthand side of the stream, guided by path sign No. 262 - Hathersage. Gain a stile before Birley Lane with Bronte Cottage to your left. Cross to a stile and continue descending gently to the edge of Brookfield Manor (Conference Centre). The path bears left past the car park area and onto Baulk Lane. Turn right and descend lane eventually passing your earlier path and Riverside. Retrace your steps past the Cricket Field and right down Besom Lane to the main road. Cross over and pass the Methodist church back to the car park.

The summit of Win Hill.

WIN HILL - 462m, LOSE HILL - 476m & MAM TOR - 517m.

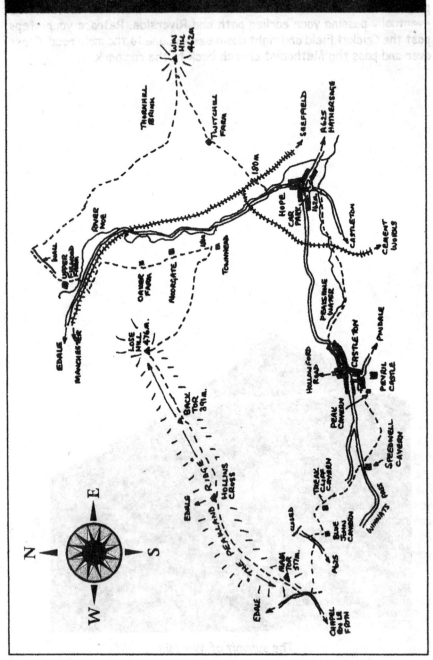

WIN HILL - 462m
- LOSE HILL - 476m
and MAM TOR - 517m
via The Peakland Ridge
- 666m of ascent
- 14 miles/23km.
- allow 5 to 6 hours.

ROUTE - Hope - Killhill Bridge - Twitchill Farm - Win Hill - Roman Road - Upper Fulwood Farm - Oaker Farm - Moorgate Guest House - Townhead - Lose Hill - Back Tor - The Peakland Ridge - Hollins Cross - Mam Tor - Blue John Cavern - Treak Cliff Cavern - Speedwell Cavern - Peak Cavern - Castleton - Peakshole Water - Hope.

- 1:25,000 Outdoor Leisure Map No. 1 - The Dark Peak - East Sheet.

- Central Hope.

- Old Hall Inn, Hope. Several in Castleton.

- Hope Chest, Hope. Blue John Cavern. Numerous in Castleton.

ABOUT THE PEAKS AND WALK - The ultimate peak bagging walk of the Peak District! However many times I do it, I am still enthralled by the views. One of my earliest recollections of walking in the Peak District was with a small group one winters day huddled around a primus stove making a brew on the wooded slope of Back Tor - those **WERE** the days! You climb all the peaks and traverse the ridge from Lose Hill to Mam Tor which I call The Peakland Ridge. It is busy in summer but don't let put you off. You also walk past the four caverns of Castleton and there are many refreshment places on the final section back to Hope. From leaving Hope you should be on the summit of Win Hill in 45 mins; 2.20 hours at Lose Hill; 2.30 at Back Tor and 3.0 hours to Mam Tor!

WALKING INSTRUCTIONS - From Hope car park turn right then left along the Edale Road. In 1/4 mile turn right along a lane and cross Killhill Bridge over the River Noe and follow the lane towards the railway line, passing footpath sign No. 122 - "Win Hill via Twitchill". Walk through the railway bridge and turn right onto a track. Follow the track which soon swings left and begin ascending to Twitchill Farm, more than 1/4 mile away. Pass the main farm on the left to a stile and continue ascending to a stile and onto another. Continue ahead on the ascending path eventually come out on the ridge before the rocky summit of Win Hill. Turn right and ascend to the summit and views, especially up the Woodlands Valley. Retrace your steps back to the ridge and continue along it, soon with a wall on your left to a stile. Continue slowly swinging right heading north westerly along the spine of the hill slowly descending past Wooler Knoll to your right. 1 1/2 mile from the summit join the Roman Road from Navio, Brough, and continue to a stile. Over this turn left over another stile and keep a wall on your left as you descend to a stile. Continue down to a ladder stile and soon bear slightly left to walk past Upper Fulwood Farm with a National Trust Information Centre. Continue along the track and cross Bagshaw Bridge over the River Noe. Immediately afterwards bear right and ascend the path to the Edale Road, gained via a stile.

Cross to your right and walk through a railway tunnel and ahead along the start of Fiddle Clough. In a few yards turn left to a stile and keep a wall on your left. The path soon swings right to a stile and wall on your left - you are now heading southwards. Continue to another stile and past Oaker Farm on your left to a stile. Now on a tarmaced surface soon pass Moorgate Guest House (Countrywide Holidays) on your left. Less than 1/4 mile later a lane from your right joins yours and turn right up it towards Townhead. Before it turn right over a stile and ascend the path/track as you begin your ascent of Lose Hill, a mile away. The path is well defined and follow it all the way to Lose Hill summit and view point. Along the ridge is Mam Tor your eventual goal.

Turn left along the stone slabs heading westerly to Back Tor. Here descend steeply at first before walking along the ridge of Barker Bank to the cross roads of path at Hollins Cross, and view indicator dedicated to Tom Hyett of the Long Eaton Rambling Club. Now you begin ascending again heading for the summit of Mam Tor about 3/4 mile away, your highest point of the route. Descend the stone slabbed path down to the road at Mam Nick and turn left over a stile. Bear left following the National Trust path signed for Blue John Cavern. The path soon keeps close to a wall on your left to the closed road near the cavern. Turn left and then right to Blue John Cavern. On its left is a ladder stile. Over this follow the path to a stile and begin a delightful high level traverse around the slope to Treak Cliff Cavern. Walk past on the right and turn right to continue beside a wall on your left on a path to a stile and onto another before the Winnats Pass road and Speedwell Cavern. Cross to a stile and National Trust property - Long Cliffe. Follow the path beside the wall on your left round to a gate. Continue into Castleton with Peak Cavern and Peveril Castle to your right. Cross the road bridge and ascend the lane past Douglas House on your left to the Market Place and YHA on your left. Cross to your far left and walk down Back Street past the church on your left to the main road (A625).

Follow it straight ahead and around to your right (How Lane) passing two inns. Nearing the end of the village turn right onto a track signposted No. 35 - Hope - 592 ft. Follow the track to a stile and it now becomes a well defined path with a sewage works to your left. Afterwards the path bears left with Peakshole Water to your left. The path is well stiled and leads to the railway line to Hope Cement Works. Cross over and continue on the path above the Water to the Hope road beside path sign No. 36. Turn left and pass Hope's well preserved Pinfold and bear left past Hope Church on your right to the A625 road. Turn left back to the car park.

Back Tor.

KINDER LOW - 633m

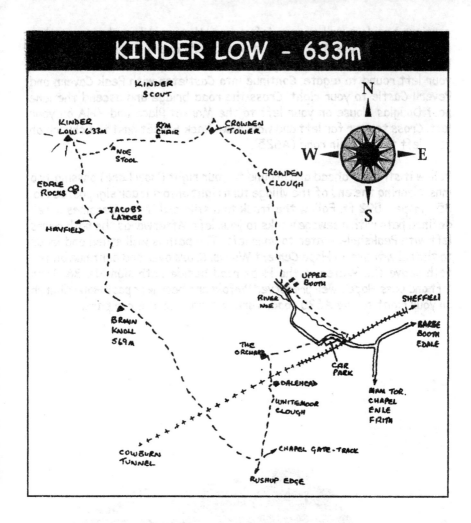

KINDER
SCOUT

KINDER
LOW - 633m

RYN
CHAIR

CROWDEN
TOWER

NOE
STOOL

CROWDEN
CLOUGH

EDALE
ROCKS

JACOBS
LADDER

HAYFIELD

N
W E
S

UPPER
BOOTH

RIVER
NOE

SHEFFIELD

BARBE
BOOTH
EDALE

BROWN
KNOLL
569m

THE
ORCHARD

CAR
PARK

MAM TOR.
CHAPEL
EN LE
FRITH

DALEHEAD

WHITEMOOR
CLOUGH

CHAPEL GATE - TRACK

COWBURN
TUNNEL

RUSHUP EDGE

Summit of Kinder Low - 633m.

KINDER LOW
- 633m
and Brown Knoll 569m
-500m of ascent
- 9 miles / 15 km
- allow 4 hours

Route - Barber Booth - Upper Booth - Crowden Clough - Crowden Tower - Pym Chair - Kinder Low - Edale Rocks - Brown Knoll - Whitemoor Clough - The Orchard - Barber Booth.

 - 1:25,000 Outdoor Leisure Map No. 1 - The Dark Peak - West Sheet.

 - Barber Booth. Grid Ref. SK109848.

 - None. Nearest at Edale.

 - Upper Booth.

ABOUT THE PEAK - One of the highest in the Peak District! A steep climb onto the Kinder Plateau near Crowden Tower - about an hours walk! Half an hour later you should be at the cairn and trig point on Kinder Low! In a further 1/2 hour you should be on top of Brown Knoll - 569m. And 1 1/2 hours later back at the car park! This is a magnificent circuit of the Upper Booth valley. The views are magnificent; especially south and west-wards.

WALKING INSTRUCTIONS - From the car park walk down the road - eastwards - to the railway viaduct and turn left over the footbridge over the River Noe. A few yards beyond turn left on a track to a stile. The pathline is now a defined path and well stiled to the hamlet of Upper Booth, 1/2 mile away, reached via a gate. Turn left past the buildings to the road and turn right. A few yards later turn right over a stile by a footpath sign, into Open Country. The path keeps to the lefthand side of Crowden Brook to a footbridge. Then on the righthand side to a stile and the ascent begins. The path keeps near to the brook and often fords it. High up the path divides - one keeps to the brook bed and involves scrambling in places. The other ascends steeply to the right of Crowden Tower. Whichever route you take turn left at the top for Crowden Tower, walking along the southern edge of Kinder Scout. Beyond the tower you enter the fascinating gritstone boulder area of the Wool Packs. Continue on the path to Pym Chair and onto the solitary stone - Noe Stool.

Here the path descends but rather than lose height soon bear right aiming for Kinder Low - 633m. Nearing the "summit" you join a path to its peaty location. After admiring the view descend the path past Edale Rocks and then beneath Swine's Back down to the bridleway from Jacob's Ladder. Cross over to the stile and follow the stone slabbed path leading towards the summit of Brown Knoll - 569m. The path turn right then left for the summit. From the summit head south-easterly on a defined path - your goal is towards Rushup Edge 1 1/2 miles away. In more than 1/2 mile the path divides; keep to the lefthand one around the edge of the plateau. In more than 1/4 mile to your left on the southern slopes of Horsehill Tor can be seen a cairn - erected for the National Trust in memory of John Charles Gilligan by his family. Continue on the faint path leading round, eventually by a small wall on your left to a path sign No. 98 - By Dalehead to Upper Booth - and the Chapel Gate Track.

Don't go down the track, turn left and descend steeply down the path to Whitemoor Clough and a footbridge. Cross and continue on to Dalehead - you cross on the lefthand side of the building, but to your right is a National Trust Information Centre. Continue on the path to The Orchard Farm and turn right along the drive - a Concessionary path to the road close to the car park. Keep straight ahead to it.

Brown Knoll's summit.

View up Crowden Brook to Crowden Tower.

BLEAKLOW HEAD - 633M

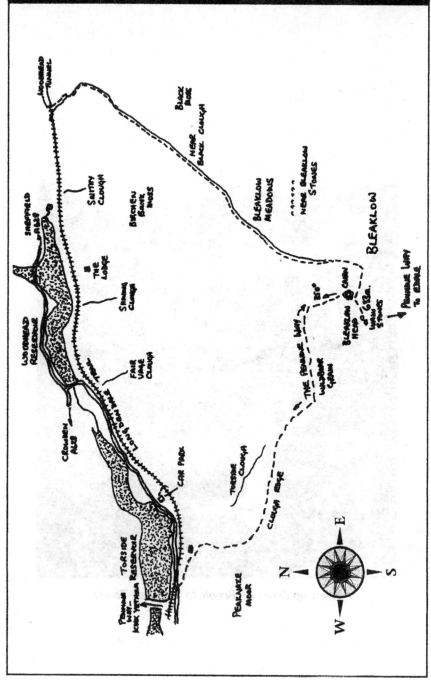

BLEAKLOW HEAD
- 633m
- 400m of ascent
13 miles / 20 km
- allow 5 to 6 hours.

Route - Torside Reservoir Car Park - Longdendale Trail - Woodhead Tunnel - Near Black Clough - Black Clough - Cairn - Wain Stones - Cairn - Pennine Way - Wildboar Grain - Clough Edge - Reaps - Longdendale Trail - Car Park.

- I 25,000 Outdoor Leisure Map No. 1 - The Dark Peak - West Sheet.

- Close to Longdendale Trail off the B6105 road. Grid Ref. 069983. There are toilets here and an Information Centre (open weekends only).

- None - carry what you need. Seasonal refreshments in car park.

ABOUT THE PEAK AND WALK - A great day's walk in high moorland with beautiful views. I saw no one on the day I did it except for a lone Pennine Way walker! Choose a clear settled day for although the path is mostly defined it is still wise to use a compass and carry one. It is not a dramatic summit - just the highest point of the peat moorland and Peak District - but the walk up Black Clough is exceptional and the descent along the Pennine Way above Torside Reservoir is a rewarding "mountain" walk. You also walk a major section of the Longdendale Trail which forms part of the E8 Trans Pennine Walk from Liverpool and Hull AND onto Istanbul more than 2,500 miles away - I hope to walk it some day! You walk the trail first as a lull before the ascent. There are paths above Black Clough but it is more exciting to scramble up the base of the clough. You will no doubt see many and startle red grouse. In winter no doubt the mountain hares. In August the heather is full bloom and cloudberry grows substantially. Have a good walk and enjoy one of the finest "peaks" of the Peak District.

WALKING INSTRUCTIONS - From the car park walk up to its top lefthand corner to the path to the Longdendale Trail. Gaining the trail turn left and basically keep on the trail for more than 3 miles to the entrance to Woodhead Tunnel. After a mile pass the site of Crowden Station; in use from July 1861 to February 1957. At the Woodhead tunnel turn right along the track towards the A628 road but before it turn right over a bridge over the River Etherow to a stile on your left. Over this keep the river on your left as you walk along a track. Follow the track round to your right with the river on your left and pass some delightful ponds. Keep ahead as the track becomes a path and soon cross the stream to your left then right to keep walking up the base of the steep sided clough. There is a small path and basically choose you way using either side of the stream as the terrain dictates. After half an hour you are past the steepest part as the clough widens and the sides decline in size as you gently ascend. About 3 1/2 miles from the tunnel entrance and approximately 1 1/2 hours of walking you will be high on Bleaklow. Keep beside the stream bed following it to a fence and stile. Continue following the widest channel as it curves right (westwards) towards the large cairn on Bleaklow Head. This is almost the highest point but 200 yards to the south-west is a stake and the Wain Stones at the highest point. After your visit return to the large cairn and as written on a rock are now on the Pennine Way (350°).

The path is well defined now and in 1/4 mile the path swings left - almost due west - and descends Wildboar Grain. Cross the stream and continue on the Pennine Way as it keeps high above Torside Clough along Clough Edge. At the end descend steeply to a stile and continue on the path towards the farm - Reaps - and then keep left on the farm drive to near the Glossop road. Before it turn right, as signed and right again onto the Longdendale Trail. Keep on the trail for 3/4 mile to the path to the car park. Turn left and retrace your steps back to it.

Longdendale Trail - Crowden Station.

Near Black Clough.

Wain Stones.

65

BLACK HILL - 582m

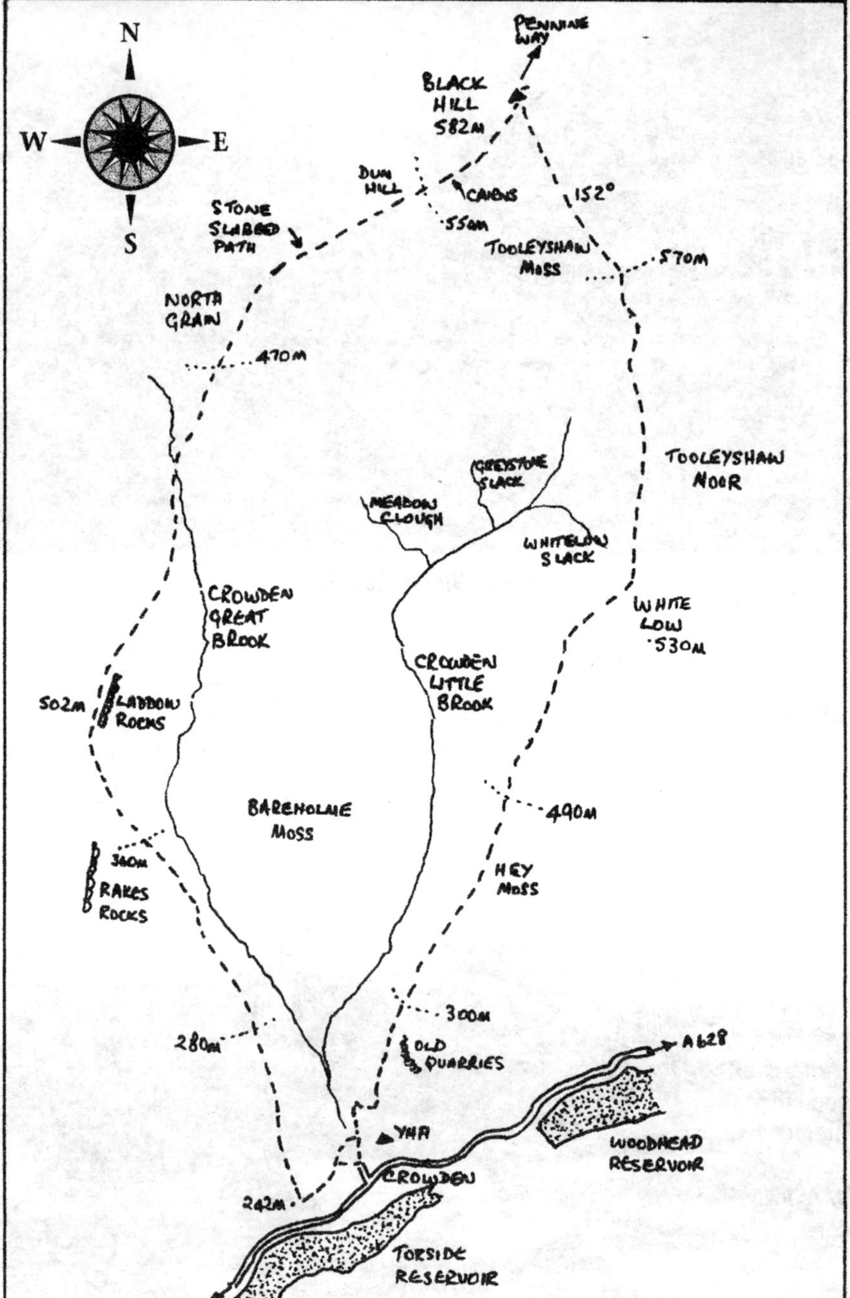

N
W — E
S

PENNINE WAY

BLACK HILL 582m

DUN HILL

CAIRNS 550M

152°

STONE SLABBED PATH

TOOLEYSHAW MOSS

570M

NORTH GRAIN

470M

GREYSTONE SLACK

MEADOW CLOUGH

WHITELOW SLACK

TOOLEYSHAW MOOR

CROWDEN GREAT BROOK

WHITE LOW 530M

502M

LADDOW ROCKS

CROWDEN LITTLE BROOK

360M

RAKES ROCKS

BAREHOLME MOSS

490M

HEY MOSS

280M

300M

OLD QUARRIES

A628

YHA

WOODHEAD RESERVOIR

CROWDEN

242M

TORSIDE RESERVOIR

A628

BLACK HILL
- 582m
- 380 m of ascent.
- 10 miles / 16 km
- allow 4 hours

Route - Crowden Car Park - Pennine Way - Laddow Rocks - Dun Hill - Black Hill - Tooleyshaw Moor - White Low - Hey Moss - Crowden.

-1:25,000 Outdoor Leisure Map No. 1 - The Dark Peak - West sheet.

- Crowden. Just off the A628 road. Grid Ref. SK072893.

- None. Be self contained.

ABOUT THE PEAK AND WALK - Renowned for its "boggy" summit and a major obstacle on the Pennine Way. I am pleased that the hand of man has not stretched this far - although you do walk along a stone slab route towards the peak - and the summit area is still a black oozy area. Unless during a dry summer you still need determination to actually reach the triangulation pillar that now sticks way above the surrounding peat. On my latest visit I had to almost encircle it before finding a "safe" passage to the pillar. The "hill" is aptly named with the whole area black oozing peat! You will no doubt meet Pennine Wayers on your ascent as they start their second day towards Kirk Yetholm. Choose a fine day for in bad weather the summit is a wild and desolate area. A compass is an essential item, even in fine weather. Whilst not being a lofty summit it is still a good ascent to it with extensive views on the ascent and descent to Bleaklow and the Longdendale Valley.

WALKING INSTRUCTIONS - Exit the car park via its bottom righthand corner, following the signed path to the toilets. Gaining the track beside them turn right and pass the campsite on your left and at the top turn left along the track following the Pennine Way. At the junction the route ahead is your return route. Follow the track over Crowden Brook to a gate and 150 yards later turn right at the path sign - Pennine Way and Black Hill. The path leads to a stile and onto a ladder stile at the boundary of Open Country with a memorial cairn to Harry Phillips, a keen rambler, erected by the Manchester Ramblers in 1980. Continue ascending on the distinct path to the top of Laddow Rocks nearly 1 1/2 miles away. Continue along the top of the rocks with Crowden Great Brook below. The path descends gently to near the brook before ascending gently again. Ahead can be seen the stone slabbed path that curves up the slope of Dun Hill, nearly 2 miles from Laddow Rocks. Beyond the hill you come to a large cairn before walking across the peat to the summit of Black Hill - about 1 3/4 hours of walking from the car park.

From the summit the direction at first is not obvious because of the flat peat and groughs landscape. Go on compass bearing 152° to a stile about 1/4 mile away and once over the pathline becomes more defined and at first is well cairned as you cross Tooleyshaw Moss. You descend then ascend gently over Tooleyshaw Moor before descending slightly and ascending White Low. Here the path turns right and in 1/2 mile gain a large cairn on the edge of the high ground. Descend more steeply taking the "middle" path which soon descends to a track. Keep ahead on the track and pass the large boulders of former quarry activity on your left. Reach a stile on the boundary of Open Country. Descend the path to another stile and track. Turn right to a ladder stile and follow the track to your left to the path junction you reached at the start. Keep straight ahead retracing your steps past the campsite on your right to the toilets and left into the car park.

View to Hey Moss and your return route.

Stone flagged path towards Dun Hill.

Summit of Black Hill.

69

MARGERY HILL - 546m
and OUTER EDGE - 541m.

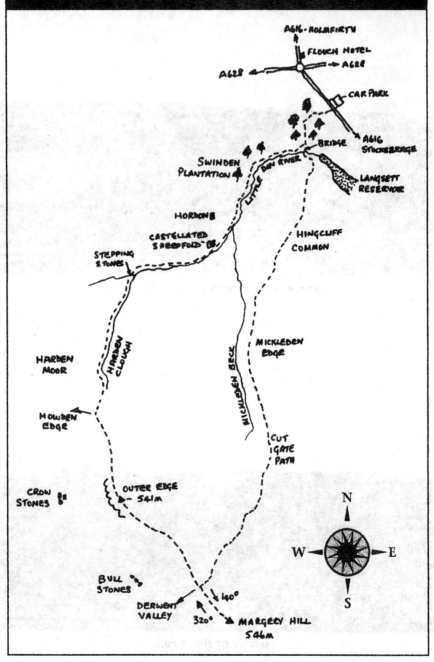

MARGERY HILL
- 546m
and OUTER EDGE
- 541m
- 400m of ascent
- 11 miles / 18 km
- allow 5 hours

Route - Flouch Car Park (A616) - Crookland Wood - Hingcliff Common - Mickleden Edge - Cut Gate Path - Cut Gate - Margery Hill 546m - Cut Gate - Outer Edge - 541m - Harden Clough - Little Don River - Crookland Wood - A616.

- 1:25,000 Outdoor Leisure Map - The Dark Peak - East Sheet.

- 1/4 mile south of Flouch Hotel - Yorkshire Water Langsett (Flouch) Car Park just off the A616 road. Grid Ref. SK202013.

- None. Nearest in Flouch or Langsett. Carry what you need.

ABOUT THE WALK AND PEAKS - A wonderful moorland walk! First you walk through pine trees to the Little Don River before starting the gradual ascent along the Cut Gate Path past Mickleden Edge to the cairn on Howden Edge. Here you turn left to ascend Margery Hill - 546m. You return to the cairn and cross moorland to the trig point on the summit of Outer Edge - 541m. You descend the other side having once more admired the views - especially to Mam Tor. 1/2 mile of walking you turn northwards and descend a delightful path down Harden Clough to the Little Don River. You follow this back to the pine trees - a particularly attractive section - and retrace your steps back to the A616 and car park. A truly exceptional day out in quiet moorland - I only saw two people - in the distance - all day!

WALKING INSTRUCTIONS - Exit the car park via the top righthand corner - as signed near an Information board. Cross the A616 road to a track and bridlepath sign. Keep straight ahead into the pine trees. Follow the track for less than 1/4 mile to the next path sign. Turn left here still on a track and pass another bridlepath to your left - the path on your right is your return path. Keep ahead and in a few yards bear right and descend the track to the bridge over the Little Porter River with Langsett Reservoir to your left. Follow the track round to your left then right as you ascend to Open Country. Keep straight ahead and in 1/4 mile pass a track to your left at spot height 322m. Keep ahead across Hingcliff Common as the track now becomes a path. In 3/4 mile pass another Open Country sign as you continue on the path onto Mickleden Edge with Mickleden Beck below on your right. In a further 1/4 mile pass the Peak District Footpath preservation Societies Footpath plaque No. 50 dated 1925. This sign has stood here over seventy years - doesn't it make sense to make the present day signs the same way, rather than wood which last a few years?

Keep ahead gently ascending - Cut Gate Path - for more than two miles to the cairn on the edge of Howden Edge - Cut Gate. Here the views unfold southwards over Kinder and the Hope Valley - Mam Tor looks spectacular from here! Turn left - 140° - and in little over 1/4 mile reach the triangulation pillar on the summit of Margery Hill - 546 m. Margery Stones are just ahead. Retrace your steps back to the cairn - 320°. Continue on this bearing to cross moorland - the path is defined and sometimes staked - and in less than a mile gain the triangulation pillar on the summit of Outer Edge - 541 m. As you walked to your left were the Bull Stones and Crow Stones Edge. Continue on the path heading northwards as you descend gently. In more than 1/4 mile pass a boundary stone with the letter R on. 300 yards later pass another and in a few yards turn right and walk along the lefthand side of Harden Clough. The path is not obvious at first but in 100 yards as you descend along the lefthand side of the clough it becomes well defined. You are in Open Country. In more than a mile reach the bottom with stone walled fields ahead and Hordron Clough to your left. Cross the Little Don River via the stepping stones and turn right. Keep the river on your right as you follow a small path. In 1/4 mile pass on your left an impressive castellated sheepfold. In another mile turn left then right to continue on the lefthand side of the river. 1/4 mile later gain a bridlepath sign and Open Country sign. Go through the stile and turn right following a path beside a wall with the river below on your right. Descend to the river and walk through pine trees to a stile. Continue on the path which soon brings you to your start out path/track. Turn left along it and then right to regain the A616 road. Cross over to regain the car park.

The summit of Margery Hill.

The summit of Outer Edge.

BACK TOR - 538 m

STEPS

GREEN SITCHES

LOST LAD

TRACK

SHOOTING BUTTS

FAR DEEP CLOUGH

BACK TOR - 538m

DERWENT EDGE

CAKES OF BREAD

PIKE - LOW - 405m

WALL

DOVESTONE TOR

LANEHEAD

SALT CELLAR

WELLHEAD

SITE OF DERWENT VILLAGE

WHITE TOR - 487m

WHEEL STONES

TRACK

GRAINFOOT CLOUGH

DERWENT

A0SCAR

LADYBOWER RESERVOIR

DERWENT

A0SCAR

CROOK HILL - 374m

FAIRHOLMES

ASHOPTON VIADUCT

DINE BANK FARM

A57 SHEFFIELD

GLOSSOP A57

N

W — E

S

CAR PARK

A6013 BAMFORD

BACK TOR
- 538m
- 350 m of ascent
- 9 miles / 15 km
- allow 4 hours.

Route - Ashopton Viaduct - Ladybower Reservoir - Derwent Village Site - Wellhead - Lanehead - Pike Low - Green Sitches - Lost Lad - Back Tor - 538 m - Cakes of Bread - Derwent Edge - Dovestone Tor - Salt Cellar - White Tor - Wheel Stones - Whinstone Lee Tor - Ashopton - Ashopton Viaduct.

- 1:25,000 Outdoor Leisure Map No 1 - The Dark Peak - East Sheet.

- Roadside on A57 before Ashopton Viaduct. Grid Ref. SK196865.

- Nearest Ladybower Inn on A57, 1/2 mile east.

ABOUT THE PEAK AND WALK - I had began this book at Thorpe Cloud and over the next month headed northwards climbing the peaks with Back Tor as my last one. I felt quite sad for it had been a great series of walk, but I cheered up knowing that Back Tor was one of my favourites and the walk along Derwent Edge is still a stunning walk. The view from here and Back Tor is 360° and you can see many of the "Peaks" of the Peak District, so it makes a fitting end. The weather too was kind - dull on setting out and moments later the sun broke through to create an unforgettable scene. I walked it all in clear blue sky and after I reached the car park the clouds rolled in, as though a curtain had come down. First you walk beside Ladybower Reservoir to the site of Derwent village. Here you leave the reservoir and start climbing up via Lanehead onto the moors. You walk around Far Deep Clough with views to the triangulation pillar on Back Tor. You ascend steeply to the cairn and panorama plaque on Lost Lad before continuing to the gritstone bouldered summit of Back Tor. From here it is all down hill along Derwent Edge past fascinating outcrops to Whinstone Lee Tor. Here you descend into pine trees to Ashopton and the car park. A fitting end to the climbs.

WALKING INSTRUCTIONS - From the car park walk beside the road to the start of the Ashopton Viaduct and turn right up the lane towards the remaining houses of Ashopton - you walk down here at the end. In a few strides at the righthand corner, as footpath signed, keep left and walk along the track on the righthand side of Ladybower Reservoir. The first mile is through mostly pine trees but after 1/2 mile you pass some fine beech trees. Leaving the trees behind at Grainfoot Clough and continue for another 1/2 mile to the site of Derwent village - a notice board details where the houses stood. Continue on the track round to your left and ascend the now tarmaced surface. At the top turn right, as footpath signed, and enter National Trust property - Wellhead. In 100 yards reach the farm buildings and bear left and continue ascending on a well stiled path as you ascend to Lanehead Farm (National Trust). Continue ascending on a track up Briery Side and get your first glimpse of Back Tor to your north-east. Reach a stile and continue on a grass track which is well footpath signed as you approach Pike Low (National Trust). Keep on the track with a wall on your right and head towards a small pine plantation. Before it bear left, as signed, still on the track and at the next path sign, bear right - Derwent Edge. The track passes grouse shooting butts. Follow the track round to your right but do not take the path on your right. keep on the track now bearing slightly left to the base of the hill of Lost Lad. Here ascend straight up the slope via the stone steps to the cairn and panorama plaque - in memory of W.H.Baxby 1901-1977 - a keen walker and erected by the Sheffield Clarion Ramblers. The plaque gives the direction of many of the "peaks" in this book. Now on a stone slabbed path continue to the immediate right of the boulders of Back Tor and turn left to ascend to the triangulation pillar.

From the summit you will see the path heading southwards along Derwent Edge. Descend and follow this stone slabbed path, at first, for almost 3 miles. First pass the gritstone boulders - The Cakes of Bread - on your left. 1/4 mile later cross Dovestone Tor and nearly 1/2 mile on your right is the Salt Cellar. Continue on over White Tor - 487 m - and a 1/4 mile pass the Wheel Stones on your left. In another 1/4 mile cross the Derwent-Moscar path - Footpath sign No. 248 and continue on the edge path as it curves right to Whinstone Lee Tor nearly 1/2 mile away. Here meet another path - a bridleway from Moscar to Derwent. Leave the edge here but not on the bridlepath. Descend the path by a wall and follow it round to your left by a wall and soon into pine trees. Follow the path for 1/2 mile and descend to a gate on the edge of the plantation. Turn right and walk down the lane past Ding Bank Farm and onto your start out path. Gain the A57 road and a few yards to your left you are back at the car park.....**sadly!**

The summit of Back Tor - 538 m.

*Self portrait of the author at the Salt Cellar on his way down
from the last "peak", Back Tor.*

Climb the Peaks - Climb record -

Thorpe Cloud - 287 m ....

Ecton Hill - 369 m ....

The Roaches - 505 m ....

Wincle Minn - 385 m ....

High Wheeldon - 422 m ....

Chrome Hill - 440 m ....

Shutlingsloe - 506 m ....

Tegg's Nose - 350 m ....

Shining Tor - 559 m ....

Kerridge Hill - 313 m ....

Sponds Hill - 410 m ....

Lantern Pike - 373 m ....

High Neb - 458 m ....

Win Hill - 462 m, Lose Hill - 476 m, & Mam Tor - 517 m ....

Kinder Low - 633 m ....

Bleaklow Head - 633 m ....

Black Hill - 582 m ....

Margery Hill - 546 m & Outer Edge - 541 m ....

Back Tor - 538 m ....

I've Climbed the Peaks of the Peak District

CLIMB THE PEAKS BADGE

Complete ten climbs in this book and get the above special embroidered badge and signed certificate. Badges are white cloth with lettering and logo embroidered in four colours.

BADGE ORDER FORM

Date climbs completed...

NAME ....

ADDRESS ....

....

Price: £3.00 each including postage, VAT and signed completion certificate. Amount enclosed (Payable to *Happy Walking International Ltd*) ..

From: **Happy Walking International Ltd.,**
Unit 1, Molyneux Business Park, Darley Dale,
Matlock, Derbyshire. DE4 2HJ
Tel /Fax (01629) - 735911

********** *YOU MAY PHOTOCOPY THIS FORM* **********
"HAPPY WALKING!" T SHIRT
- Yellow (Sunflower) with black lettering and walking man logo.
Send £7.95 to *Happy Walking International Ltd.*, stating size required.
John Merrill's "Happy Walking!" Cap - £3.50
Happy Walking Button Badge - 50p inc p & p.

LONG CIRCULAR WALK GUIDES

LONG CIRCULAR WALKS IN THE PEAK DISTRICT Vol. 1 - Fifteen carefully selected long walks to illustrate the scenic variety of the Peak District. Each walk is between 10 and 20 miles long— some easy, some hard—starts from a car park, has a detailed map and instructions with history notes, and includes a pub. 64 pages 16 maps 45 photographs ISBN 0 907496 42 3 £5.50

LONG CIRCULAR WALKS IN THE PEAK DISTRICT Vol. 2 - Fifteen more walks throughout the Peak District, between 10 15 miles long. 50 pages. 15 maps. 12 photographs. ISBN 1 874754 £5.50

LONG CIRCULAR WALKS IN THE PEAK DISTRICT - Vol. 3 - Ten more walks between 9 and 21 miles long. All new routes on little used paths to some of the finest unspoilt areas of the National Park. Many explore the eastern are, while others traverse the northern moors and limestone dales; a fitting addition to the series! ISBN 1 874754 47 0. 56 pages. 10 maps. 12 photographs. £4.95.

LONG CIRCULAR WALKS IN THE STAFFORDSHIRE MOORLANDS - 15 circular walks 10 to 20 miles long - based on Longnor, Flash, The Roaches, Tittesworth Reservoir, Biddulph Moor, Butterton, Alstonefield, Wettonmill, Onecote, Longsdon, Ilam, Waterhouses, and Consall. 76 pages. 14 maps. ISBN 0 907496 98 9   £5.50

CIRCULAR WALKS ON KINDER AND BLEAKLOW - The definitive walk guide to the moorland areas of the Peak District. 17 walks between 7 and 40 miles long; including the classic walks - Marsden to Edale (25 miles) and the Derwent Watershed Walk (40 miles).
Perfect bound and sewn, 20 maps, 46 photographs, 88 pages. ISBN 0 907496 59 8 £5.95

CIRCULAR WALKS TO PEAK DISTRICT AIRCRAFT WRECKS by John D. Mason - 9 circular walks in the Dark Peak area - Kinder and Bleaklow - to all major wreck sites. 68 pages. 35 photographs. 10 maps. ISBN 0 907496 94 6   £5.50

LONG CIRCULAR WALKS IN CHESHIRE - 12 walks between 10 and 18 miles long in Cheshire. Including sections of the Sandstone and Gritstone Trails and the Salter's Way. The walks are truly from the plains to the hills. ISBN 1 874754 14 4. 64 pages. 12 maps. 24 photographs. £5.50

LONG CIRCULAR WALKS IN NOTTINGHAMSHIRE - 10 walks 14 to 23 miles long throughout the county, including Sherwood Forest. ISBN 1 874754 22 5. 56 pages. 10 maps. 18 photographs. £4.95.

LONG CIRCULAR WALKS IN SOUTH YORKSHIRE - 10 walks 14 to 20 miles long throughout the county from the moorlands of the Peak District to the "fens" near Doncaster.
ISBN 1 874754 65 9. 52 pages. 10 maps. 9 photographs. £4.95

THE HIGH PEAK TRAIL - Several short and long walks along the trail and neighbouring area, including an end to end walk. Very detailed history notes. ISBN 1 874754 11 X. 40 pages. 8 maps. 10 photographs. £3.95

THE TISSINGTON TRAIL - (Peak District) - Several short and long walks along the trail and neighbouring area and an end to end walk. Includes very detailed history. ISBN 1 874754 10 1. 32 pages. 6 maps. 8 photographs. £3.95.

THE MONSAL TRAIL & OTHER DERBYSHIRE TRAILS. Walks on the Monsal Trail, Sett Valley Trail, Five Pits Trail and Rawthorne Trail. ISBN 1 874754 17 9. 48 pages. 12 maps. 18 photographs. £3.95

OTHER JOHN MERRILL BOOKS FROM
Happy Walking International Ltd.,

CIRCULAR WALK GUIDES -
SHORT CIRCULAR WALKS IN THE PEAK DISTRICT - Vol. 1,2 and 3
CIRCULAR WALKS IN WESTERN PEAKLAND
SHORT CIRCULAR WALKS IN THE STAFFORDSHIRE MOORLANDS
SHORT CIRCULAR WALKS - TOWNS & VILLAGES OF THE PEAK DISTRICT
SHORT CIRCULAR WALKS AROUND MATLOCK
SHORT CIRCULAR WALKS IN "PEAK PRACTICE COUNTRY."
SHORT CIRCULAR WALKS IN THE DUKERIES
SHORT CIRCULAR WALKS IN SOUTH YORKSHIRE
SHORT CIRCULAR WALKS IN SOUTH DERBYSHIRE
SHORT CIRCULAR WALKS AROUND BUXTON
SHORT CIRCULAR WALKS AROUND WIRKSWORTH
SHORT CIRCULAR WALKS IN THE HOPE VALLEY
40 SHORT CIRCULAR WALKS IN THE PEAK DISTRICT
CIRCULAR WALKS ON KINDER & BLEAKLOW
SHORT CIRCULAR WALKS IN SOUTH NOTTINGHAMSHIRE
SHIRT CIRCULAR WALKS IN CHESHIRE
SHORT CIRCULAR WALKS IN WEST YORKSHIRE
WHITE PEAK DISTRICT AIRCRAFT WRECKS
CIRCULAR WALKS IN THE DERBYSHIRE DALES
SHORT CIRCULAR WALKS FROM BAKEWELL
SHORT CIRCULAR WALKS IN LATHKILL DALE
CIRCULAR WALKS IN THE WHITE PEAK
SHORT CIRCULAR WALKS IN EAST DEVON
SHORT CIRCULAR WALKS AROUND HARROGATE
SHORT CIRCULAR WALKS IN CHARNWOOD FOREST
SHORT CIRCULAR WALKS AROUND CHESTERFIELD
SHORT CIRCULAR WALKS IN THE YORKS DALES - Vol 1 - Southern area.
SHORT CIRCULAR WALKS IN THE AMBER VALLEY (Derbyshire)
SHORT CIRCULAR WALKS IN THE LAKE DISTRICT
SHORT CIRCULAR WALKS IN THE NORTH YORKSHIRE MOORS
SHORT CIRCULAR WALKS IN EAST STAFFORDSHIRE
DRIVING TO WALK - 16 Short Circular walks south of London by Dr. Simon Archer Vol 1 and 2
LONG CIRCULAR WALKS IN THE PEAK DISTRICT - Vol.1,2 and 3.
WHITE PEAK AIRCRAFT WRECK WALKS
LONG CIRCULAR WALKS IN THE STAFFORDSHIRE MOORLANDS
LONG CIRCULAR WALKS IN CHESHIRE
WALKING THE TISSINGTON TRAIL
WALKING THE HIGH PEAK TRAIL
WALKING THE MONSAL TRAIL & OTHER DERBYSHIRE TRAILS
40 WALKS WITH THE SHERWOOD FORESTER by Doug Harvey
PEAK DISTRICT WALKING - TEN "TEN MILER'S"
CLIMB THE PEAKS OF THE PEAK DISTRICT

CANAL WALKS -
VOL 1 - DERBYSHIRE & NOTTINGHAMSHIRE
VOL 2 - CHESHIRE & STAFFORDSHIRE
VOL 3 - STAFFORDSHIRE
VOL 4 - THE CHESHIRE RING
VOL 5 - LINCOLNSHIRE & NOTTINGHAMSHIRE
VOL 6 - SOUTH YORKSHIRE
VOL 7 - THE TRENT & MERSEY CANAL
VOL 8 - WALKING THE DERBY CANAL RING
WALKING THE LLANGOLLEN CANAL

JOHN MERRILL DAY CHALLENGE WALKS -
WHITE PEAK CHALLENGE WALK
DARK PEAK CHALLENGE WALK
PEAK DISTRICT END TO END WALKS
STAFFORDSHIRE MOORLANDS CHALLENGE WALK

THE LITTLE JOHN CHALLENGE WALK
YORKSHIRE DALES CHALLENGE WALK
NORTH YORKSHIRE MOORS CHALLENGE WALK
LAKELAND CHALLENGE WALK
THE RUTLAND WATER CHALLENGE WALK
MALVERN HILLS CHALLENGE WALK
THE SALTER'S WAY
THE SNOWDON CHALLENGE
CHARNWOOD FOREST CHALLENGE WALK
THREE COUNTIES CHALLENGE WALK (Peak District).
CAL-DER-WENT WALK by Geoffrey Carr,
THE QUANTOCK WAY
BELVOIR WITCHES CHALLENGE WALK
THE CARNEDDAU CHALLENGE WALK

INSTRUCTION & RECORD -
HIKE TO BE FIT.....STROLLING WITH JOHN
THE JOHN MERRILL WALK RECORD BOOK

MULTIPLE DAY WALKS -
THE RIVERS'S WAY
PEAK DISTRICT: HIGH LEVEL ROUTE
PEAK DISTRICT MARATHONS
THE LIMEY WAY
THE PEAKLAND WAY
COMPO'S WAY by Alan Hiley

COAST WALKS & NATIONAL TRAILS -
ISLE OF WIGHT COAST PATH
PEMBROKESHIRE COAST PATH
THE CLEVELAND WAY
WALKING ANGELSEY'S COASTLINE.

CYCLING Compiled by Arnold Robinson.
CYCLING AROUND THE NORTH YORK MOORS .
CYCLING AROUND MATLOCK.
CYCLING AROUND LEICES & RUTLAND.
CYCLING AROUND CASTLETON & the Hope Valley.
CYCLING AROUND CHESTERFIELD.
CYCLING IN THE YORKSHIRE WOLDS
CYCLING AROUND BUXTON.
CYCLING AROUND LINCOLNSHIRE.

PEAK DISTRICT HISTORICAL GUIDES -
A to Z GUIDE OF THE PEAK DISTRICT
DERBYSHIRE INNS - an A to Z guide
HALLS AND CASTLES OF THE PEAK DISTRICT & DERBYSHIRE
TOURING THE PEAK DISTRICT & DERBYSHIRE BY CAR
DERBYSHIRE FOLKLORE
PUNISHMENT IN DERBYSHIRE
CUSTOMS OF THE PEAK DISTRICT & DERBYSHIRE
WINSTER - a souvenir guide
ARKWRIGHT OF CROMFORD
LEGENDS OF DERBYSHIRE
DERBYSHIRE FACTS & RECORDS
TALES FROM THE MINES by Geoffrey Carr
PEAK DISTRICT PLACE NAMES by Martin Spray

JOHN MERRILL'S MAJOR WALKS -
TURN RIGHT AT LAND'S END
WITH MUSTARD ON MY BACK
TURN RIGHT AT DEATH VALLEY
EMERALD COAST WALK

SKETCH BOOKS -
SKETCHES OF THE PEAK DISTRICT

COLOUR BOOK:-
THE PEAK DISTRICT.......something to remember her by.

OVERSEAS GUIDES -
HIKING IN NEW MEXICO - Vol I - The Sandia and Manzano Mountains.
Vol 2 - Hiking "Billy the Kid" Country. Vol 4 - N.W. area - " Hiking Indian Country."
"WALKING IN DRACULA COUNTRY" - Romania.

VISITOR GUIDES - MATLOCK . BAKEWELL. ASHBOURNE.

Join the
Happy Walking Club
.... only £10 per year!

A unique club.

One years subscription entitles you to -

* All books ordered from Happy Walking International Ltd - POST FREE

* Books by John Merrill autographed free

* Badges and Certificates - £2.50 each

* Regular information on new books

* Information on John Merrill's latest marathon walk

* Advance notice of John Merrill's lectures

* 10% discount on purchases made at John Merrill's Happy Walking Shop - on production of membership card

* Membership card is valid for twelve months from date of joining; renewable on anniversary date.

• •

Yes, I would like to join the Happy Walking Club. I enclose herewith £10 for a year's subscription, made payable to Happy Walking International Ltd. (If paying by credit card please complete the additional form overleaf, thank you)

Name _____

Address _____

_____

Membership No. _____

Happy Walking Order Form

		qty/size
	Happy Walking T Shirt Sunflower Yellow with logo and lettering in black. All sizes - £7.95p inc p & p	
	Happy Walking Cap Black with yellow lettering. One size fits all. - £7.95p inc p & p.	
	Happy Walking Mug White with green lettering. £4.50p inc postage.	
	Happy Walking Pen - £0.50p inc p& p	
	Happy Walking Key Ring - £0.50p inc p& p	
Happy Walk club Membership - £10.00p		

We accept - VISA, MASTERCARD, AMEX, SWITCH

Card No. ☐☐☐☐ ☐☐☐☐ ☐☐☐☐ ☐☐☐☐ ☐☐☐☐

Exp date ☐☐ ☐☐   Issue No ☐☐ ☐☐

Amount ....Signed ....

Name ....

Address ....

....

Post Code .... Tel No. ....